CW00361614

BARCELONA

BY
JUDY THOMSON AND
ROGER WILLIAMS

Produced by
Thomas Cook Publishing

Written by Judy Thomson and
Roger Williams
Original photography by Gavin Harrison
Original design by Laburnum Technologies
Pvt Ltd

Editing and page layout by
Cambridge Publishing Management Ltd
Unit 2, Burr Elm Court, Caldecote CB3 7NU
Series Editor: Karen Beaulah

Published by Thomas Cook Publishing
A division of Thomas Cook Tour Operations Ltd

PO Box 227, The Thomas Cook Business Park
Units 15–16, Coningsby Road
Peterborough PE3 8SB, United Kingdom
E-mail: books@thomascook.com
www.thomascookpublishing.com
Tel: +44 (0) 1733 416477

ISBN-13: 978-1-84157-545-2
ISBN-10: 1-84157-545-3

Text © 2006 Thomas Cook Publishing
Maps © 2006 Thomas Cook Publishing

First edition © 2003 Thomas Cook Publishing
Second edition © 2006 Thomas Cook Publishing

Head of Thomas Cook Publishing: Chris Young
Project Editor: Linda Bass
Production/DTP Editor: Steven Collins

Printed and bound in Spain by: Grafo Industrias Gráficas, Basauri.

Cover design: Liz Lyons Design, Oxford.
Front cover credits: Left © Travelstock 44/Alamy; centre © Visual & Written SL/Alamy;
right © Johner/Photonica
Back cover credits: Left © Getty Images; right © Thomas Cook Tour Operations Ltd

C o n t e n t s

KEY TO MAPS	
Ⓜ	Metro
ⓘ	Information
★	Start of walk
A7	Road number

Introduction

Barcelona is the largest and most exciting port city in the Mediterranean. It basks in a nest of hills in the northeast corner of Spain, with its back to Madrid and its eyes on the sea that gave it, in parts, a glorious past.

Down by the port

Formal, mercantile, medieval – the city's past reverberates in the dank canyons of the old town and in the vast dockyards that today form the maritime museum. Add to this a creativity of spirit that was responsible for some of the finest Romanesque art in the world as well as the great 19th-century *modernista*

A detail of the Columbus monument

buildings of Gaudí and others, and you arrive at a dazzling mix of old and new, a place that never lacks the courage of its convictions. Reticence and shyness are strangers here.

Spain's second city has for nearly two centuries been the industrial, money-making part of the country, though the textile industry that brought wealth to the early arts patrons such as Eusebi Güell declined significantly in the 1980s. It is still rich, however, producing 20 per cent of the country's GDP, and people continue to arrive from all over Spain looking for work. Its popular coasts – the Costa Brava to the north and Costa Daurada to the south – are also places where people come to find work.

Cultural Hothouse

From this vibrant background have come first-rate art and culture, from opera singers and film directors to painters, designers and architects, all of whom are accorded great respect. Its cultural institutions – the Picasso Museum, Liceu opera house and museums of Romanesque and contemporary art – are world-class. Much of the entertainment is out in the streets, however, and few cities offer the visitor so much to see by doing nothing but simply wandering around.

The People

Two opposite poles are at work on the Catalan psyche. *Seny* is the sensibility that produces the bourgeois traditionalist who can be seen among the elegant crowd arriving in the Rambla for the latest offering at the Liceu opera. *Rauxa* is the impetuousness that has resulted in fits of church burning, and the creativity so suited to Surrealism. In Catalans these two elements are said to live side by side.

Catalan (*català, see pp24–5*) is the first language of the city and this sets it apart from other regions of Spain. This independence has been fought for down the centuries, and native Barcelonans are still likely to see themselves as Catalans first and Spaniards second.

The Sagrada Família, Gaudí's greatest legacy

Casa Lleo-Morera, in the 'Block of Discord' – so-called because of the area's clashing architectural styles

When to Visit

The city is good for visiting year round. Winters can be cold but bright, with chilly evenings and an average temperature of 10°C (50°F). School summer holidays last three months and during July and August, when temperatures soar, families try to escape to the hills and the coasts, leaving the city to the breadwinners and to visitors. For anyone staying more than a few days, a trip to the coast provides a welcome break, and there are also many historical sites to see inland, from Montserrat monastery to Roman Tarragona, and from medieval towns to *cava* vineyards. The ideal months to visit are May and June, or September and October, when the full heat has left the sun and the sea is still warm enough to swim in.

The City

Hard by the sea and beneath two imposing hills, Barcelona has spread into the surrounding communities, scooping up a third of the population of Catalonia, the region over which it presides. Extending from the Pyrenees to the Mediterranean, it has an abundance of natural resources that have helped to make this city of merchants and manufacturers great.

Plaça del Pi, the old town

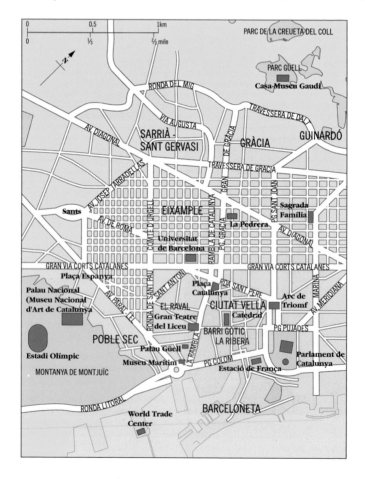

Barcelona is the capital of Catalonia, the region of northeast Spain that was conceived by the Francs in AD 850 as a buffer state against the ebbing tide of Muslims. Its founder was Guifré el Pelós (Wilfred the Hairy), the first Count of Barcelona, whose family ruled in an unbroken line for 500 years. Until 1659 the territory extended into France and as a result, with a language akin to Provençal or Langue d'Oc, it has sometimes felt more affinity with Paris than with Madrid, an upstart town set up in the centre of the peninsula in 1561 to unite the disparate regions of Spain. Rivalry between the two cities remains brisk.

Roman Foundations

Barcelona is at heart a Roman town. The Plaça St Jaume is where the forum stood and its foundations can be seen beneath the Palau Reial (*see pp46–7*). Roman walls are still visible by the cathedral and by the former royal palace, and it is easy to see how the city spread.

These walls proved insufficient by the 14th century when the nation was at the height of its expansion, and the medieval walls were built, encompassing the business quarter around the stock exchange and at first lining the Rambla, then encompassing the working district of El Raval. In the 19th century the

The Ajuntament, the city hall, in Plaça Sant Jaume where the Roman forum stood

population burst out of the walls altogether and the *modernista* Eixample ('extension', *see pp60–63*) was built.

Recent Developments

Decades of under-investment and neglect in the Franco years saved the city from too many 1960s' high-rise developments. When investment did come, it arrived in a magnificent rush for the 1992 Olympic Games, and the infrastructure was bulldozed into the 21st century with breathtaking panache, thanks to men of vision such as the architect Oriol Bohigas and the city mayor, Pasqual Maragall, a qualified town planner and now President of the Catalan government. Almost overnight, Barcelona was transformed.

It was as if the city had been waiting to awake. Ring roads went in, new Metro lines were established and the whole of the seafront, with the Olympic Port, opened up, giving the city new icons such as the Hotel Arts, one of the tallest buildings in Spain. Once the ball began to roll, it kept going, opening up new city spaces and looking up the coast past the Olympic developments to create Diagonal Mar, a new residential and business district, where the Avinguda Diagonal meets the sea and the new, invisible, city walls stretch all the way to the River Besòs. This was the site of the Forum 2004.

The Metropolitan Area

The city reached its present boundaries of 97sq km (37sq miles) in 1929 and now has a population of 1.7 million. The metropolitan area, with an additional 2.3 million people, spreads out into surrounding towns and includes 164 municipalities and seven *comarques*. A *comarca* is a municipal area of Catalonia, ruled by a comarcal council. There are 41 altogether, divided among four provinces each named after its principal city: Barcelona, Girona, Lleida and Tarragona.

The Hills

Two hills look down on the city. By the sea is Montjuïc (213m: 700ft) on which the castle sits overlooking the busy port and the sea, with public gardens and museums tumbling around its feet. Inland is the other pleasure garden of Tibidabo (512m: 1,680ft) and the Collserola hills, a hunting ground for wild boar and mushrooms. Dotted about in between are communities that have managed to maintain a village feel, such as Sarrià and Gràcia. Each district has its own flavour, its own shops, its own feast day.

THE RHYTHM OF LIFE

The city stirs late, especially downtown where shops and even some cafés do not open until 10am. Most Barcelonans live within easy commuting distance of the city and at 2pm they hurry home to lunch, leaving the city to siesta until 4pm when another rush hour fills the streets again.

In summer, to avoid the worst of the heat, office workers may labour straight through from 8am until 3pm, when they can take off for the beach or the cool of their homes. In the hottest month, August, some work places and factories close altogether.

The Torre de Calatrava on Montjuïc, site of the 1992 Olympic Games

History

700 BC	First settlements by indigenous Iberians, the Laeitani.
300 BC	Carthaginians from southeast Spain under Hamil Barca take over the city, renaming it Barcino.
217 BC	After Barca's son, Hannibal, marches on Rome, the Romans respond by invading Spain, landing on the Costa Brava to start their conquest of the peninsula.
200 BC	Roman Barcelona established.
AD 476	After the fall of Rome, Visigoths fill the vacuum.
700	Moors cross from Africa and take over Spain, capturing Barcelona in 713. They are repulsed by the Franks who set up the *Marca Hispanica* (Spanish March).
897	Death in battle of Guifré el Pelós, first Count of Barcelona.
988	Barcelona declared autonomous after the Moors are pushed back to the south.

The royal palace in the Plaça del Rei

1137	The House of Barcelona is joined with neighbouring Aragon through marriage.
Late 13th century	The House of Catalonia–Aragon becomes a dominant force in the Mediterranean.
1359	Establishment of *Corts Catalanes*, the nation's parliament.
1395	The *Jocs Florals*, troubadour poetry competitions, are introduced during a literary flowering.
1469	Ferdinand of Aragon marries Isabella of Castile (the Catholic Monarchs), uniting the two major houses of Spain.
1492	Moors expelled from Spain, Jews outlawed.

Columbus reaches America and returns to Barcelona with Carib Indians to be baptised in the cathedral. Trade with the New World is denied to Barcelona, however, leading to its decline.

1659	The Treaty of the Pyrenees concludes the Thirty Years War between Spain and France, ceding all Catalan territories north of the Pyrenees to France.
1714	In the War of the Spanish Succession, Barcelona backs the House of Habsburg, but the Bourbons are victorious. After a 13-month siege, the city falls on 11 September (*La Diada*), a national day in Catalonia. The *Corts* are abolished, the language banned, and a citadel (La Ciutadella) is built to police the city.
1808	Barcelona is taken by Napoleonic troops in the War of Independence.
1814	After peace is restored in Europe, Barcelona flourishes, becoming the industrial powerhouse of Spain, introducing steam to power its textile mills.

1833	Start of the protracted Carlist Wars, instigated by the pretender, Don Carlos.
1835	Many religious houses closed and land redistributed.
1848	Mainland Spain's first train operates between Barcelona and Mataró.
1854–6	La Ciutadella is pulled down along with the city walls as the population explodes.

The magnificent façade of Santa Maria del Mar

1859	The *Renaixença* (Renaissance) of Catalan, with a revival of the *Jocs Florals*.
1860	The new city (Eixample) is designed by Ildefons Cerdà.
1888	The Universal Exhibition is held in the Parc de la Ciutadella, and the *modernista* style of architecture is celebrated.
1901–2	General strike by city workers.
1909	*Setmana Tràgica* (tragic week): widespread rioting and destruction of religious houses.
1923	Catalan aspirations thwarted by the dictatorship of Primo de Rivera.
1929	A second Universal Exhibition is held on Montjuïc, where the Poble Espanyol and other lasting architectural curiosities are built.
1931	Under the Second Republic Catalonia is granted its first statute of independence.
1936–9	The Spanish Civil War begins after Nationalist

insurgents under General Franco attack the Republic. Barcelona holds out to the end, but falls with little fighting. Hundreds of thousands flee into France. Lluis Companys, president of the Generalitat, is executed with thousands of others in the castle of Montjuïc. Catalan is banned.

1940s– 1950s	Shunned by the bulk of the international

The main cathedral's 'Gothic' front completed in the 19th century

community, Spain starves in the *Noche Negro* (black night) after the war.

1952	Spain accepts financial aid and allows US bases in the country.
1960s	Thousands of immigrants, mainly from the south, arrive looking for work, and shanty towns are thrown up around the city.
1975	Death of General Franco celebrated with free *cava* in the streets. Catalan is a recognised language again.
1979	Statute of Autonomy gives Catalonia some independence.
1992	Olympic Games held after a massive six-year restructuring and rebuilding programme.
1994–2000	New cultural centres open.
2004	Forum 2004 sees the city extended north to the River Besòs.
2005	Tourism booms. Mayor Clos announces new beaches for 2007. The Catalan government presents new Statute to Madrid in a bid for more independence.

THE CATALAN FLAG

The legend behind the design of the shield and flag of Catalonia is that it was a grant of arms from Charles the Bald, grandson of Charlemagne and King of the West Franks. In 897 he was doing battle with the Moors near Lleida when, in answer to a summons, Guifré el Pelós (Wilfred the Hairy), the first Count of Barcelona, came to his aid. Wilfred's intervention turned the course of the battle, but in his finest hour he was slain. As he lay dying Charles dipped his fingers in the count's blood and dragged it across his golden shield, thus inventing *Les Quatre Barres*, the four bands of the Catalan flag.

The magic fountain and Palau Nacional on Montjuïc

Governance

The city is governed from the heart of the old town in Plaça St Jaume where the flags of Spain, Catalonia and Barcelona fly. The Ajuntament (town hall) is in the Casa de la Ciutat, flanked by statues of local dignitaries and city police (the Guardia Urbana). Facing it across the cobbled square is the Palau de la Generalitat, home of the regional government, guarded by the autonomous police force (the Mossos d'Esquadra) and the figure of the patron saint of Catalonia, St George.

Flags flying above the Generalitat

Spain is a constitutional monarchy ruled over by King Juan Carlos who has been on the throne since the restoration of the monarchy in 1975. The country is governed from the Cortes (parliament) in the capital, Madrid. The king appoints a prime minister from the party with the majority of seats in the Chamber of Deputies, the lower house, to which 350 members are elected by proportional representation every four years. An upper house contains the Senate, with 49 members from each of the 17 autonomous regions of Spain. Catalonia is one of these.

The Generalitat

The autonomous region of Catalonia is governed by the Generalitat in Barcelona. For nearly a quarter of a century it was dominated by the conservative Convergència i Unió party under the charismatic presidency of Jordi Pujol.

The fact that the Generalitat, representing the country as well as the towns, has always been under conservative control, while the Ajuntament, representing the more radical view of the city, has during this time been in socialist hands, leads to inevitable clashes. In 1999 the elected socialist mayor Pasqual Maragall tried to break this mould by challenging Pujol for the Catalan presidency. He was unsuccessful, and was succeeded in the mayor's office by his deputy, Joan Clos i Matheu, who won a four-year term in 1999 and was re-elected in 2003.

Council meetings are held in the Saló de Cent, a magnificent Gothic hall built in the golden reign of Pere III (1336–87) for the city's original Council of a Hundred. It is only occasionally open to the public.

The elected members of the Generalitat sit in the Parlament de Catalunya, in a building which was once the Arsenal of the 18th-century citadel, in the Parc de la Ciutadella.

Rights and privileges

The autonomy won from Madrid is relatively new, but for centuries, first under the count-kings of Barcelona and then under civic rulers, Catalonia was an independent nation that governed itself. Its parliament, the Corts Catalanes, was formally established in 1359 to represent the nobility, church and people and to regulate the city's finances and ensure its rights.

These rights, or *usatges*, were of fundamental importance to Catalans, and each time they have been threatened there has been trouble. In trying to shake free from Madrid, Catalonia has sided with France against Spain, to its cost. The last time it declared independence was in 1931 under the Republican leader of the Generalitat, Francesc Macià. It lasted less than a day.

There are Catalans today who want a complete break with Madrid, notably the underground organisation Terra Lliure (free land), but autonomy has taken the edge off their demands.

The Catalan Parliament building in Parc de la Ciutadella

Catalans are clearly sentimental about traditions like the *sardana*, the national dance, banned by Franco and danced clandestinely, or Montserrat, the 'Sawn Mountain', the spiritual centre of Catalonia. But Catalan nationalism, this feeling of a separate identity which crosses all social and political divides, has much deeper roots. A quick look at history shows why. Long before Spain existed as a state, Catalonia was a nation with its own government, laws and institutions, its own bickering feudal lords, semi-legendary dashing warrior rulers with outlandish names, imperial glory days and dynastic ructions.

The government, the Generalitat de Catalunya, existed in the 13th century, and the Barcelona Corts was one of the earliest parliaments in Europe.

In the 8th century, a cluster of counties with a common sense of identity emerged as a buffer state between Charlemagne's Christian empire and Moorish Spain. In 878 Wilfred the Hairy united several counties and proclaimed himself Count of Barcelona, and the embryonic Catalonia soon asserted its independence from the Frankish kings.

When the County of Barcelona was united with the Kingdom of Aragon by marriage in 1137, each people kept its own language, laws and institutions. Catalonia–Aragon – known as the Crown of Aragon – pushed south and east. By the 13th century, Barcelona rivalled Genoa and Venice as a maritime power, ruling over an empire that included Sicily, Sardinia, Naples and Athens.

But with the marriage of Ferdinand II of Aragon to Isabella of Castile, Catalan power began to wane. While Portugal and Holland emerged with independence from the War of the Spanish Succession (1701–13), Catalonia was occupied and severely punished by the victorious Philip V. An entire Barcelona neighbourhood was razed to build a citadel, on the site of what is now the Parc de la Ciutadella. All Catalonia's institutions were abolished, its universities closed, its

modernisme for which Barcelona is so well known. Catalonia's limited Statute of Autonomy and political voice during the second republic was short-lived, as Spain sank into chaos and finally civil war. With Franco's victory in 1939, Catalonia was punished once again. Resistance simmered underground. Two years after Franco's death, the Generalitat was provisionally restored. On 11 September 1977, one million Catalans staged a massive demonstration to demand the re-establishment of the Statute of Autonomy. This was ratified in October 1979, giving Catalonia a measure of home rule as an 'autonomous community' within the Spanish state.

Today many of Catalonia's aspirations have been achieved, although the industrious Catalans, who contribute the lion's share to the public purse, are ever watchful of the centralising and retrograde forces perceived to emanate from Madrid. In the face of globalisation, Catalonia now promotes itself as a dynamic pluralist society embodying justice, equality and sustainability, an innovative force in the new Europe.

language banned: it became an outlying province of the new centralist Spanish state. Catalonia neither forgave nor forgot. The fall of Barcelona on 11 September 1714 is still solemnly commemorated today.

In the mid-19th century the Catalan economy took off with the industrial revolution, and Catalonia soon became the most enterprising and prosperous region of Spain. The *Renaixença* (Renaissance) movement to restore Catalan culture and language gained momentum. The effervescence of the period is embodied by the fabulous

Left: The Catalan flag flies alongside the Spanish flag
Above: The revival of traditions like 'Castells' has been ardent since Franco's death (Castellers of Barcelona)

The Gran Teatre del Liceu

Culture

One of the great attractions of Barcelona is that its art, architecture and culture are closely woven into its everyday bustle. A lively cosmopolitan arts scene, exuberant Mediterranean festivals and a notable work ethic combine to give the city a unique flair.

Barcelona is a city of worldwide architectural fascination, with layer upon layer of history built into its urban fabric: the remains of the Roman walls and the soaring Catalan Gothic of the basilica of Santa Maria del Mar, the

Dazzling interior of Domènech i Montaner's Palau de la Música

heady flights of *modernisme* and the far-reaching urban redevelopment of the 1980s and 1990s. As well as the must-see buildings by Gaudí and his contemporaries, a walk around the Eixample offers more private glimpses of *modernista* vestibules and shops. Barcelonans are extremely proud of their cultural heritage, which they feel is part of their identity. Shopkeepers, for example, lovingly conserve and display antique cash registers, sewing machines and ceramic jars.

Another salient example of the cultural texture of Barcelona life is the World Heritage-listed Hospital de la Santa Creu i Sant Pau, which has the distinction of being a fully operational 21st-century teaching hospital. Linking up with the spirit of the *modernista* movement, one of the key ideas underpinning the pre-Olympic urban renewal was the 'monumentalisation' of the outlying neighbourhoods and their promotion as centres of culture: this was the rationale behind sculptures like Claes Oldenburg's giant *Matches* up in the Vall d'Hebron, and, more recently, the building of the Teatre Nacional and the Auditori (and a shopping centre, of course) in a hitherto derelict area close to one of the city's main traffic nexus.

Museums

Barcelona is also famed for its large number of museums: ethnology, maritime, decorative arts, footwear, automata, geology, perfume... as well as highlights like the Picasso Museum and the world's finest collection of Romanesque art at the Museu Nacional d'Art de Catalunya. In addition to the permanent displays, there is always a wide choice of temporary exhibitions at the Museu Picasso, the Fundació Joan Miró, the Fundació Antoni Tàpies, the MACBA, the Pedrera and the Caixa Fòrum, amongst others.

Theatre and dance

Vibrancy is a word much bandied about when talking about Barcelona, and it is no less applicable to the performing-arts scene. Barcelona has a long tradition of theatre, which is now flourishing, both in the range and quality of productions and in the number of theatre-goers. Many small theatres across the city stage classic works in translation as well as contemporary plays. The Teatre Nacional de Catalunya takes a new look at classical theatre, both national and international, stages the latest in contemporary theatre productions, and hosts multidisciplinary events and dance performances. As its name suggests, the Mercat de les Flors theatre used to be Barcelona's flower market. Dance plays a major part in its stimulating programme which features many international visiting groups. In fact Barcelona has

Sardanes are danced religiously every Sunday in the Cathedral Square

The Camp Nou football stadium – pride of all 'Barça' fans

developed a first-class reputation for innovative contemporary dance, with a number of small and medium-sized companies, such as the Companyia Gelabert-Azzopardi, now enjoying international prestige. First-rate Spanish dance and flamenco companies also regularly visit.

Music

There is a tremendous variety of music to be enjoyed in Barcelona, from classical symphonies to opera, ballet, jazz, flamenco, pop, rock, indie and experimental music. Concerts, recitals and festivals abound. In recent years contemporary and experimental music has been promoted with events such as the Sonar Advanced Music Festival, the BAM (Barcelona Acció Musical) for independent music, the Jazz Festival and the Guitar Festival. The new Auditori, designed by Rafael Moneo, is now the focal point for the city's musical events and is home to the Barcelona Symphony Orchestra. In addition, it stages seasons such as Ibercámera with many visiting orchestras and soloists and offers a full programme of all kinds of music including jazz, world music and flamenco. The Orfeo Catalá choir is the flagship survivor of the patriotic and sociocultural movement of the late 19th century, when over 150 choral groups were founded in Catalonia. It gives numerous concerts every year as well as acting as choir to the Barcelona Symphony Orchestra and others. Badly damaged in a fire in 1994, the Liceu opera house has been rebuilt and upgraded and offers a full programme of opera, ballet, concerts, recitals and performances for children.

Exciting venues

Venues like the fabulous Palau de la Música Catalana are worth seeing whatever is on the bill. And what a

Palau de la Música

pleasure it is to glide up into the quiet fragrant pines of Montjuïc on the escalators from Plaça Espanya and see the city spread out below, on one's way to a concert at the Palau Sant Jordi, now an integral part of Barcelona's skyline. Inside it is incredibly light and airy, even when packed to capacity for the likes of Bruce Springsteen, Bon Jovi or Paul McCartney.

Festival del Grec

The culmination of the performing arts calendar is the Festival de Barcelona Grec (Grec Summer Festival), the city's biggest performing arts festival held in late June and July. This was originally staged at the neo-Greek amphitheatre on Montjuïc, hence the name. The amphitheatre is now joined by other venues around the city, although the Grec itself is delightful on a hot summer's night. One of Europe's biggest arts festivals, the Grec offers national (Castilian and Catalan) and international theatre, dance (mainly contemporary), and music for all tastes, especially Brazilian and flamenco.

WORKING BARCELONA

Barcelonans definitely subscribe to the work ethic – they are hard-working and punctual and greatly prize efficiency – but festivals such as the Festa Major de Gràcia, the Dia de Sant Jordi and the Mercè (see pp22–3) show that they are still a Mediterranean people. They are innovative and traditional at the same time. One unique 'performance' that should not be missed is the dancing of the sardana, the intricate national dance of Catalonia, every Sunday at noon in front of the cathedral, accompanied by a traditional band called a cobla. It's democratic: if you want to join in, just enter the circle.

The Barcelona Stock Exchange in Passeig de Gràcia

Festivals

Barcelonans have a special flair for combining work, fun and creative imagination. The northern-style work ethic is by no means at odds with Mediterranean vibrancy, as the city's exuberant red-letter days show.

Open-air venue in the summer festival

Cavalcada dels Reis (Three Kings Parade)

5 January

Fantastically colourful procession on the eve of Epiphany. The Three Kings or Wise Men arrive from the Orient by boat, are welcomed on the quayside (Moll de la Fusta) by the mayor, parade around the city with their retinues hurling tons of sweets into the crowd, then take presents to sleeping children.

Carnestoltes (Carnival)

Late February/early March

The final outburst of pagan indulgence before Lent. City-wide partying and processions, fireworks, dancing in Plaça Catalunya, concerts. It is business as usual in this commercially minded city: the traders in the Boquería and other markets keep on trading – in fancy dress.

Dia de Sant Jordi – Dia del Llibre (Book Day)

23 April

A memorable day for Catalans, blending fun and romance, culture and hard-headed business sense. Sant Jordi (St George) is the patron saint of Catalonia, and his feast day, which is also the anniversary of Cervantes' death, is celebrated by exchanging gifts of books and roses. The day, however, is not a public holiday, so the festivities blend in with daily life. Booksellers set up stalls in the streets complete with buckets of red roses (a discount of 10 per cent is given on all books), book launches and author signings are scheduled, and at night the usual partying takes place – dances, discos, fireworks. Benefits are also organised, such as book collections for hospitals.

St George's day – Dia del Llibre

Fira de Sant Ponç

11 May
Feast day of the patron saint of beekeepers and herbalists: stalls selling honey, herbs, candied fruit and other natural products in Carrer Hospital in the heart of the old city. Colourful and very, very fragrant.

L'Ou Com Balla (The Dancing Egg)

Corpus Christi–early June
The Dancing Egg is a very old custom: a previously emptied egg is left to 'dance' on the jets of the fountain in the cathedral cloister and other courtyards in the Gothic Quarter: Casa de l'Ardiaca, Ateneu Barcelonès, Museu Frederic Marès. The fountains are decorated with flowers, making it one of the most curious and picturesque traditions in the city's folklore.

Nit de Sant Joan, Nit de Foc (St John's Night)

Night of 23/24 June
The most obviously pagan of all the festivals, marking the summer solstice.

Explosive celebrations on the night of Sant Joan

A wild night of fireworks and partying, although the traditional bonfires have been banned from the city. Impressive formal firework displays, live music, dancing, *cava* flowing on the Rambla. Revellers wind up on the beach at sunrise. Of course, 24th June is a public holiday.

Festa Major de Gràcia (Gràcia Annual Fete)

Mid-August
Vibrant neighbourhood festival (*see pp72–3*) offering non-stop open-air entertainment for all ages and tastes. The Festa kicks off with giants and castle-builders and goes out, literally, with a bang: a massive and spectacular firework display.

La Diada de Catalunya

11 September
Catalonia's National Day (*see pp16–17*). Public holiday. A solemn occasion for political demonstrations and the laying of wreaths on monuments to the fallen, rather than for festive celebrations.

Festes de La Mercè

Week around 24 September
A week-long extravaganza centred around the feast day of Barcelona's patroness, Our Lady of Mercy. The Mercè has everything – processions, giants, castle-builders, fire dragons, music of all kinds, free-entry days at museums, visual and performing arts shows, craft and food fairs, fireworks and the associated Contemporary Music Festival and Barcelona Alternative Music Festival.

It may well come as a surprise to the visitor to hear Barcelona people speaking a sharp staccato tongue or to see what looks like a jumble of Spanish, French and Italian on street signs and restaurant menus: *entrada* (entrance), *sortida* (exit), *museu* (museum), *ciutat* (city), *església* (church), *pa* (bread), *carn* (meat), *vi* (wine) and so on. This is Catalan, the official language of Catalonia alongside Castilian (Spanish), according to the Spanish Constitution of 1978.

Spoken by over six million people and understood by ten million (in Catalonia, Valencia, the Balearic Islands, Roussillon in southern France, Andorra, and Alghero in Sardinia), Catalan is not a dialect, as is often mistakenly assumed, but a fully-fledged language derived from the Latin spoken in northeastern

Spain during the Roman empire. It is therefore a sister language to Spanish, French, Italian and Portuguese. It boasts a cultural and literary tradition dating from the 12th century, with its own literary Golden Age in the 15th century. In that period trade flourished and Catalan was used as a lingua franca throughout the Mediterranean. It was also honed into a first-rate literary language: Joanot Martorell's novel of chivalry *Tirant lo Blanc*, published in 1490, was read and praised by Cervantes.

But later two attempts were made to wipe out the language. Philip V severely punished Catalonia for fighting against him in the War of the Spanish Succession, and from 1714 abolished all its institutions, closed its universities and banned the language. The late 19th

century and early 20th centuries saw a great revival, the Renaixença, which was curtailed by the Spanish Civil War.

Under Franco's repressive regime, Catalan was banned entirely from public use and an entire generation of Catalans grew up unable to read or write their mother tongue. Artists and writers, scientists and scholars flocked into exile. The poignant 1962 novel, *La Plaça del Diamant*, set in Barcelona's Gràcia neighbourhood during the Spanish Civil War, was written by Mercè Rodoreda in exile in Switzerland and has been translated into more languages than any other Catalan work; its title in English is *The Time of the Doves*.

Since the granting of the Statute of Autonomy in 1979, the government of Catalonia has vigorously implemented a policy of 'linguistic normalisation' designed to promote Catalan as an ordinary working language in all walks of life: education, the media, the arts, science and technology, business, public administration, the courts. As a result, Catalan now seems to be in excellent shape, happily co-existing with Castilian. Most Barcelonans are bilingual and slip automatically back and forth between the two languages depending on who they are talking to. Courtesy and consideration rule, and very few are such extreme nationalists that they will refuse to speak Castilian to non-Catalan speakers. Many writers and journalists, actors, singers and TV presenters work in both languages, and the main Spanish language papers publish supplements in Catalan. One popular paper, *El Periódico*, publishes a daily edition in each language. Catalan has two TV channels and numerous radio stations. It has its rock bands, websites and incomprehensible teenage slang, its crime thrillers, poetry and pop psychology bestsellers, its TV chat shows and soap operas.

While non-Catalan speakers claim they are discriminated against on the job market, the Catalans insist that 'positive discrimination' is crucial to prevent degeneration into a local patois. They still fear for the future of their language: the long shadows of Philip V and General Franco still lurk in the Catalan collective unconscious.

Left: The Barcelona Manifesto on Rambla Catalunya
Above: Barcelona's main Catalan newspaper

Impressions

If you drink the waters of the famous Font de Canaletes in La Rambla, legend has it you will fall in love with the city and inevitably return. According to the no less uncertain science of statistics, Barcelona has invariably come out in the top five European cities as a favourite destination, best place to open a business, or for its superior quality of life. Few visitors, whether on a bargain break, romantic escapade or business trip, can resist its charms. Maybe the waters of the fountain are to blame. Whatever it is, Barcelona's undeniable magnetism makes people return.

Foster's communication tower pricks the Collserola hills

When to visit

Such is Barcelona's new popularity that flights and hotels fill with great alacrity, especially over peak periods like Christmas, Easter and European summer holidays. So do La Rambla, the Sagrada Família, the Picasso Museum and other key tourist sights. The beaches are crammed with locals at weekends

The city lies densely between the Collserola hills and the Mediterranean

from mid-June to mid-September. So if you have the choice of travelling out of season it is recommended: there are fewer crowds and the flights are correspondingly cheaper. Besides, Barcelona is a city for exploring on foot, observing street life and architecture, visiting museums and savouring long lunches – all of which are better without blistering heat. The ideal time is spring or autumn, though as perfect weather can never be guaranteed you could be equally lucky in the middle of December, often characterised by crisp sunny days.

Areas of the city

Getting a grip on the basic layout of Barcelona and deciding which parts you want to visit is easy. Looking at a city map you can see how it lies between the Collserola range and the sea, enclosed by the hill of Montjuïc and the River Besòs. The identifiable labyrinth of narrow streets between Plaça Catalunya and the

Santiago Calatrava's bridge

port is the Ciutat Vella (Old Town) which includes the Gothic quarter.

The contrastingly geometrical grid of streets which spreads between the Ciutat Vella and the former villages of Sants, Sarrià, Gràcia and Horta is the Eixample, built according to Ildefons Cerdà's extension plan in the mid-19th century. The heart of the Eixample contains some of the finest *modernista* buildings. This was like a new town, built to cope with the expanding population bursting out of the old city walls.

Climbing up the hills are either smart residential districts or (further away from the centre) denser, humbler residential areas where cheap housing was thrown up to cope with the influx of immigrants from other parts of Spain in the 1950s and 1960s. The waterfront comprises the huge industrial port, the new marinas and 4km of beaches stretching to the River Besòs, where a neglected wasteland has been converted

into the Forum leisure and conference centre (*see pp58–9*). Just behind the beaches are the districts of Barceloneta, Vila Olímpica, Poble Nou (a 19th-century industrial area, part of which was razed to build the Olympic Village in 1992), and the newest residential and commercial zone of the city, Diagonal Mar.

Beyond Barcelona

For anyone here for longer than a week the city is happily easy to get out of. The suburbs just behind the Collserola range are readily accessible by local trains managed by the Generalitat (FGC), as is the hilltop village of Vallvidrera and the surrounding woods. RENFE, the national train service, has local and regional trains serving the coastal strip north and south and beyond to the Pyrenees.

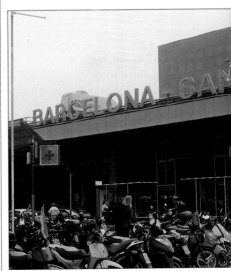

Public transport (or motorbike ...) is the best way to get around Barcelona

A walk down La Rambla is a good starting point

Where to begin

It is nearly all worth exploring, but do not attempt to do everything on a first visit. One of the joys of Barcelona is to wander around observing small details, corner shops, a market stall, a Romanesque arch, a human statue, the speedy Catalans, or to linger in a medieval patio listening to the trickle of a fountain, or at a pavement café watching the colourful world go by. Absorb the real atmosphere of this Mediterranean city by just being in its midst.

To get an overall picture of the place without risking total exhaustion the official tourist bus is a good option (*see* *Practical Guide, p187*). Its three routes cover the key spots, so you can leap off when something interests you, or identify places you want to return to. Alternatively, get a bird's-eye view from the cable car across the port on a clear day: identify the layout of the city while enjoying the peace of the ride and keeping the kids happy.

How to get around

Barcelona is manageable on foot, though a combination of walking and the excellent public transport system is best. Avoid driving at all costs unless you are aiming to keep stress levels high. Local drivers are in a hurry and know where they are going, so they have little patience for outsiders trying to cut across five lanes of traffic while looking at maps. Besides, parking is problematic. The metro (underground), bus and city trains (FGC) are efficient, and good value. You can transfer from one to another and the tram (within a reasonable space of time) on the same ticket, the multiple card T10 usable by more than one person. When all else fails the distinctive black and yellow taxis are usually at hand, and reasonably priced.

Do as the locals...

It is a personal choice, but fitting in as far as possible with the local customs and way of life can make for a more enriching visit. It does not mean generously bestowing kisses on every stranger you meet, nor a crash course in the language – but to avoid standing out as the vulnerable tourist, and becoming frustrated, try to be aware of the differences.

The Catalans are cool dressers, experts at the casual smart. They manage to wear just the right kit for the beach, but strictly for the beach, not for restaurants or church visits. When the sun shines in the winter months they may wear a lighter jacket, but never a sleeveless T-shirt. An effort to communicate in either Catalan or Spanish is well received, even if it never gets beyond *bon dia*.

Do not expect to rush round in the midday heat, shopping or sightseeing. Many shops and businesses close, even in the winter, as lunch is all-important. By eating at the same time as the locals you get a better deal: the *menu del dia* is an economic set menu offered by all restaurants, but only at lunchtimes. A short rest after the large meal will recharge the batteries so you can make the most of the late closing of shops and museums, and is essential if you want to cope with the nightlife that only gets into its stride after midnight.

You can always fall into a taxi when exhaustion sets in

Barcelona

Most of the places a visitor wants to see – and certainly more than can be conquered in a single visit – are within striking distance of Plaça Catalunya, hub of the city, which marks the divide between the old town and the new.

The large open square of Plaça Catalunya is a gathering and meeting place. Underground is a metro and main railway station, as well as a tourist office, and beside it is the city's best-known department store, El Corte Inglés.

Detail of the spire on Gaudí's Palau Güell

Seawards from here (inconveniently, Barcelona refuses to sit on any map facing north) is La Rambla, one of the great thoroughfares of the world, which should be the first street to roam, heading down to the imposing statue of Christopher Columbus and the port, where there is always something to see.

The old town...
The old town lies either side of La Rambla. The most ancient part, the Barri Gòtic, is around the cathedral and royal palace, and nothing is more gratifying than becoming completely lost in its myriad streets. On the far side of Via Laietana were the homes of the medieval nobility, such as those in Carrer Montcada, where the Museu Picasso is located. The waterfront here contains the fishing community of Barceloneta and, beyond it, the pleasure beaches and restaurant-filled Olympic Port.

On the other side of La Rambla is El Raval, the traditional working district of the city, with the startlingly modern Museu d'Art Contemporani de Barcelona (MACBA). Beyond El Raval the hill of Montjuïc rises up to the castle, passing en route a couple of other

A tiny decorative part of the huge Nativity façade of the Sagrada Família

great art institutions, the Museu Nacional d'Art de Catalunya (MNAC) and the Fundació Miró, both of which are well worth seeking out.

...and the new

The Plaça Catalunya marks the start of the Eixample, the 19th-century expansion, and this is where the *modernista* architecture lies, with Gaudí's Park Güell some distance behind his unmissable Sagrada Família. This is also where you will find designer Barcelona. Start putting on the style in the Rambla de Catalunya and Passeig de Gràcia, two of the city's most elegant streets.

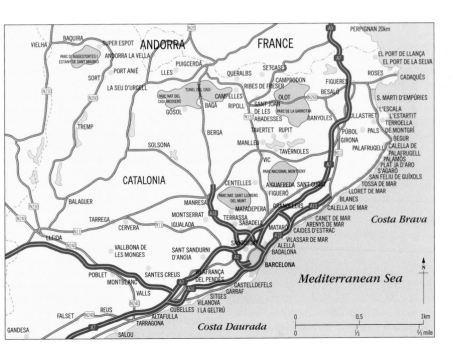

Barceloneta and the Beaches

Alphabetically, the sites of Barcelona begin with Barceloneta and the beaches that stretch north from the port towards the River Besòs. Until the development of the 1992 Olympic Games, this was the city's industrial heartland where goods trucks shunted along the shore. Now it has been reclaimed for the city's leisure and pleasure and is a particularly popular place for eating out.

Traditional lanteen-sail boat

Barceloneta, 'little Barcelona', has a flavour all of its own. This is traditionally the fishermen's district of Barcelona. Not much fishing goes on in Barceloneta's port these days, but there is still a score of boats in the fishing port by Torre de Rellotge, the former harbour lighthouse. Nearby is the Torre St Sebastià, the cable-car stop that connects to the World Trade Center in the main port and goes on up to Montjuïc. Cars leave every 15 minutes.

Barceloneta beach leads to the Olympic village and port

Displaced residents

Barceloneta was built on a grid system in a triangle of land between the Marina Port Vell and the sea to house more than a thousand people displaced from the maritime district of La Ribera – then 'the happiest quarter of Barcelona', according to the 19th-century poet Jacinct Verdaguer. In 1718, following Barcelona's defeat by the Bourbon Felipe V, the quarter had been brutally pulled down, with no compensation, to build La Ciutadella (*see pp102–3*). In fact the displaced had to wait more than a generation before the one-storey buildings went up to rehouse them. Its fifteen streets, crossed by five avenues, faced the citadel, keeping them in a line of fire so that any disturbance could easily be controlled. In the 19th century the one-storey houses gained upper floors, but there is still a harmony in these streets of small houses and breezy washing lines.

Seaside restaurants

A more recent act of brutality was the destruction of the *chiringuitos*, the shacks on the shore where afternoons could be whiled away eating fabulous seafood. This was done in the name of development, to build the new waterfront. Some new restaurants and clubs have been incorporated into the new design and together with some in the Olympic port are popular for Sunday lunch and summer evenings. Some of the old Barceloneta favourites still remain like Can Majó in Almirall Aixada 23 (*tel: 932 215 455*) which now has tables on the new designer promenade.

The restaurants that line the Avinguda Joan de Borbó on the port side of Barceloneta have long been popular, inexpensive places to eat seafood.

Socialist utopia

In fact Barcelonans have wholeheartedly embraced the new seafront. The former industrial area, Nova Icaria, named after a 19th-century socialist utopia, continues to be transformed. Some industrial buildings of Poble Nou have been snapped up as art studios and

workshops, though many have been bulldozed or converted into office space for a new technology business district, 22@. This area now merges with Diagonal Mar (*see pp58–9*).

ICARIA

Poble Nou is the former Nova Icaria, which took its name from a book by a French idealist, Étienne Cabet. Born in Dijon, Cabet went to England where he was influenced by Robert Owen and where, like Karl Marx 50 years later, he researched in the British Library. The result was *A Voyage to Icaria*, published in 1839, about a Utopian socialist society. Eight years later, a group of Icarians in Barcelona started up a journal with the slogan *Vamos a Icaria!* And that is what they did: with Cabet, a number of them set sail for America to found a new community of brotherly love. It was a disaster and Cabet died in Illinois, but the name of Icaria was given to the new industrial quarter of Barcelona.

Designer bars and restaurants line the shore

Walk: Barceloneta and the Beaches

Barcelona's beaches stretch 4.2km (3 miles) from the fishing quarter of Barceloneta to the new developments at Parc Diagonal Mar and the River Besòs. They are more crowded nearer Barceloneta and around the Port Olímpic, which is thick with restaurants and bristling with masts. This is the place to get your roller skates on, to walk the dog, or to go for a morning swim or jog.

Allow a couple of hours.

Begin at Barceloneta metro (line 4, or buses 14 and 59 from La Rambla). Return on the metro at Poble Nou (line 4).

1 Plaça de la Barceloneta

Step one block in from the Passeig Joan de Borbó beside Port Vell to find this tranquil square in the fishermen's quarter. With café tables and shady trees, it is overlooked by Sant Miquel del Port, which, like the rest of the district, was built by a military engineer, Pedro Cermeño. This explains its Baroque appearance – a style otherwise rarely seen in the city. Nearby is the Plaça del Font where the covered market operates

from 7am to 3pm Mon–Sat. The flower-covered restaurant beside it is the oldest in the district, dating from 1763.

Cross the PG Maritim de la Barceloneta to the beach.

2 Platja Sant Sebastià and Platja de la Barceloneta

Between Barceloneta and the Olympic Port, these two beaches are closest to the city and therefore the most popular. Extending 2.2km (1¼ miles), they have

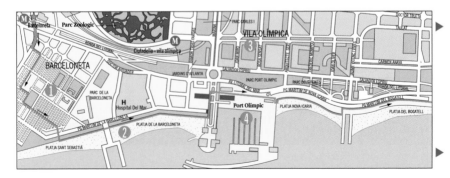

all facilities, with an information point, WCs and showers. The favourite time to swim for Barcelonans is the late afternoon, when the sand and sea are saturated with the heat of the sun that is ebbing from the day.

Turn left at the end of Barceloneta and go beyond the Port Olímpic. Vila Olímpica is the other side of Salvador Esprin.

3 Vila Olímpica

(*see pp124–5*)
Cross back over to Port Olímpic.

4 Port Olímpic

The Olympic Port is a place to watch the world sail by, from expensive yachts to capsizing beginners. It has two tiers of restaurants to choose from and at the weekend craft stalls are laid out to catch the roaring trade. An emblem of the port is the huge woven copper fish (*Pez y Esfera*) by Frank Gehry, architect of the Bilbao Guggenheim and the replacement for New York's twin towers, who was nicknamed 'fish' as a child. Gehry also figured out the 14,000sq m (150,000sq ft) of retail, commercial and maritime elements at the base of the 45-storey, 5-star Hotel Arts, designed by

The *chiringuitos* live, in a different form

Bruce Graham. The hotel has 600 rooms, 33 luxury apartments and the Barcelona Casino. Its twin, the MAPFRE building, is devoted to offices.

Continue along the beach, passing Platja Nova Icaria. At Platja del Bogatell cross the road to Parc del Litoral.

5 Parc del Litoral

This green space between the houses and the beach stands as a memento to the Olympics. Two metal sails bear an inscription to mark the opening of the new area in November 1992. La Font del Cobi has a statue of the Olympic mascot designed by Xavier Mariscal, who has one of the pioneering studios in Poble Nou.

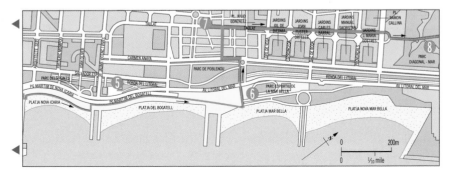

In the Plaça dels Campions are the names of the 257 gold medallists from the Olympics as well as the handprints of sporting heroes, including the footballer Pelè, the cyclist Eddie Merckx and the chess player Garry Kasparov. Beside the park are three enormous street lights 23m (75ft) tall, designed by Antoni Rosselló.
Back across PG Maritim del Bogatell, continue alongside the beach to reach Platja Mar Bella.

6 Platja Mar Bella

Twenty minutes' walk from the port across tons of imported sand, the 640m (700 yard) beach is overlooked by La Oca Mar, a restaurant in the shape of a ship with a terrace on its bow (*tel: 932 250 100*).
Cross the Av Litoral del Mar, Parc de Poblenou and Carmen Anaya to reach your next stop.

7 Rambla de Poble Nou

This is the heart of the 19th-century industrial area and there are a number of interesting former factories in the surrounding streets. There is a small-town feel to the Rambla, with a local casino and social centre halfway up. Opposite is Tio Ché (*No 44*), a handsome ice cream parlour and *orxateria*. On the right of the Rambla as you head inland is Placeta de Prim, the oldest part of Poble Nou where a plaque commemorates the idealistic 19th-century socialist Icarians (*see p33*) who lived here. The local market is held nearby in the Plaça Unió.
Walk east along Taulat, past a series of gardens, to reach Parc Diagonal-Mar.

8 Diagonal Mar

(*see pp56–7*)

All Barcelona heads for the beach; in summer early morning or late afternoon are best

Watersports in the safe Mediterranean, where the breeze is usually light

Good eating is one of the signal features of the Catalan way of life, and Catalan cuisine ranks as the best in Spain alongside the Basque, with a new generation of artistic chefs constantly dreaming up new creations. Eminently Mediterranean and based on nuts, garlic, olive oil, tomatoes, herbs and dried fruit, it reflects the diverse history of the nation, with the influences of different peoples and the varied geography of sea, plains and mountains.

The Catalans work wonders with vegetables. Sautéed with garlic, raisins and pine nuts, the much-maligned spinach is transformed into the tasty and healthy *espinacs a la catalana*, while broad beans are stewed with wine and herbs and grill-sizzled with bacon and

black pudding to become *faves a la catalana*. Salads are quintessential: crisp, light and refreshing, or almost a meal in themselves like *xató* from Sitges, which contains tuna, salt cod and anchovies and is served with piquant *romesco* sauce. Meat, chicken or rabbit *a la plantxa* (on the griddle), with *picada d'all i julivert* (finely chopped garlic and parsley) or *a la brasa* (cooked over a charcoal fire), are timelessly popular. Extra zest is provided by the garlic sauce *allioli*, or by *escalibada*, a salad of grilled and peeled aubergines and peppers. *Botifarra* is the Catalan sausage *par excellence*, popularly eaten with *mongetes* (haricot beans).

Mar i muntanya is the name of a style that blends the natural products of sea and mountain in such dishes as meat balls with cuttlefish or chicken with prawns. Another staple of the Catalan diet is *bacallà* (salt cod) which is served in innumerable incarnations: as *esqueixada*, for example (shredded raw into a salad of onions, peppers and olives), or *a la llauna* (fried then baked with tomato, red pepper, garlic and parsley).

Seafood and rice dishes abound, too. Why not try *arros negre* ('black rice' – a tasty paella made with squid and their ink) or *fideuà* (noodles cooked in fish stock)? *Suquet de peix* (fish stew) and *calamars farcits* (stuffed squid) are just two of the numerous fish dishes worth sampling. Certain pasta dishes have

become naturalised, such as *canalons*, traditionally eaten on 26 December. Mixing apparently unlikely flavours is also typical – for example, squid with chocolate, or goose with pears.

Fresh fruit is always a good option for dessert, although for the sweet-toothed, *crema catalana* (a cinnamon- and lemon-flavoured custard with a burnt sugar top) is a must. *Mel i mato* (goats' cheese with honey) and *postre de música* (mixed nuts and dried fruits) are other traditional desserts.

Catalunya also has a great pastry tradition, with a typical cake made for each and every feast day. *Panellets*, for example, are tiny marzipan cakes made for All Saints, and *coca* is a long flat pastry studded with crystallised fruits and dusted with pine nuts served at summer festivals. At Easter time, the pastissiers vie with each other to create the most elaborate chocolate sculptures.

The most famous exponent of new Catalan cuisine is Ferran Adrià, considered by some to be the best chef in the world. El Bullí, his Costa Brava culinary shrine, won its third Michelin star in 1997, one of only three restaurants in Spain with this ranking. Adrià's cooking is based on the use of fresh ingredients and gives a new twist to classic Mediterranean preparations. His philosophy of providing unexpected contrasts of flavour, temperature and texture inspires the menu of many a restaurant in Barcelona today.

Opposite: A cuisine based on produce from the sea, the plains and the mountains
Above: The healthy accompaniment to tapas – *pa amb tomàquet* – tomatoes rubbed across fresh crusty bread with a trickle of virgin olive oil

Ciutat Vella

The Old Town is the city's heart. Stretching back from the port, it encompasses the Barri Gòtic or Gothic quarter, with the cathedral and royal palace, and the Ribera district where wealthy merchants built mansions such as the ones housing the Picasso Museum. On the other side of La Rambla is El Raval, the working-class district where the city's workshops were built, and where the infamous Barri Xino (Chinese quarter) became a byword for sleaze.

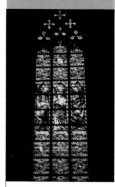

Stained-glass window, Santa Maria del Mar

Barri Gòtic

The Gothic quarter is on the site of the Roman settlement, contained within 4th-century walls, a few metres of which remain. Its excavated foundations have been exposed beneath the Royal Palace part of the City History Museum, some pillars of a temple to Augustus can be glimpsed inside the doorway of Carrer de Paradis 10 and there are a few other remnants.

A sensible starting point for contemplating the Barri Gòtic is the Plaça Nova outside the cathedral

The royal chapel is built into this section of what was the original Roman wall

and the **Portal del Bisbe**, one of the original gates leading into the old city, dating from the 1st century. This is the ecclesiastic end of town, with the **Palau Episcopal** and **Casa Ardiaca** (Archdeacon's House), where you can step into a cool courtyard, and note the delightful letterbox carved with swallows and tortoises.

You may not catch the Sunday midday *sardana* dancing in the Pla de la Seu in front of the **cathedral** (or the Thursday antiques and bric-a-brac market), but nobody visiting the cathedral should miss the cloisters, a cool spot with a pretty fountain that can be entered directly on the south side of the cathedral, in Carrer del Bisbe. The geese that rule the roost here may be a legacy of Roman times.

The Avinguda de Catedral continues to Via Laietana, where another chunk of Roman wall runs round the edge of the **Palau Reial Major**, the royal palace. Here the Plaça del Rei is a harmonious corner of the old city, with the wonderful Catalan Gothic portal of the **Palau del Lloctinent**, former home of the Spanish viceroy. But for 500 years the royal palace was the fief of the Barcelona count-kings who reigned in an unbroken line until Martí the Humanist, who gave his name to the arcaded tower in the corner which rises above the magnificent Gothic hall of the palace, the **Saló de Tinell**. It was here that Ferdinand and Isabella, the Catholic monarchs, are said to have received Columbus on his return from the Americas.

This royal complex forms part of the nearby **Museu d'Història de la Ciutat**. The Plaça St Jaume, site of the Roman forum, is today's seat of government. The **Casa de la Ciutat** (town hall) faces the **Palau de la Generalitat** (Catalan government building). The narrow streets around here seem hardly to have changed since the Middle Ages. On the Rambla side of the square is **El Call**, the old Jewish quarter. There were three synagogues in this small area. The Sinagoga Mayor has been restored and is open for visits at Carrer Marlet 5.

Between here and the Rambla is the **Plaça Sant Josep Oriol**, a lively small square to stop for a drink. Plaça del

Santa Maria del Mar, the city's finest church

Pi, which adjoins it, leads to **Carrer Petritxol**, a street of art dealers. Antique shops abound around here, but everywhere in the Barri Gòtic are delightful old shops for browsing.

El Raval

El Raval lies to the left-hand side of La Rambla as you look up from the port. It is traditionally the working-class area of the city, but its regeneration has been going on for some time, most recently with the pulling down of whole blocks to make way for a new Rambla, letting in air and light. Bars, boutiques and bookshops are now sprouting in this newly trendy area. The most spectacular innovation, however, was the **Museu d'Art Contemporani de Barcelona** (MACBA), a great slab of white designed by the American architect Richard Meier and dumped down alongside the **Casa de Caritat** (CCCB), the 18th-century house of charity, itself ingeniously turned into a cultural and exhibition space.

Charity for the workers and others was provided by the former city hospital, off the **Carrer Hospital**. Libraries and an art school occupy these medieval buildings today and the grounds are pleasant to walk through or for a snack in the small café.

The **Barri Xino**, on the waterfront side of El Raval, is not the rough area it was but some things have not changed. At the **Bar Pastis** (Carrer Santa Mónica 4) Edith Piaf has not left the turntable since 1947, and at the **Marsella** (Carrer Sant Pau 65) absinthe is still served.

Unexpectedly, there is a major Gaudí building in Carrer Nou de la Rambla. **Palau Güell**, the town house of the architect's patron Eusebi Güell, has a fascinating interior and a spectacular roof. **Sant Pere de Camp**, St Peter in the Fields, at the far end of Carrer de Sant Pau, is the only Romanesque church in the city, with some Visigothic traces. Plainsong still fills the small cloister each day.

The Picasso Museum in the Gothic Carrer de Montcada

La Ribera

This area lies on the far side of the Via Laietana and it grew to prosperity during the first major expansion of the city, from the 12th to the 14th centuries. A market and jousting field were sited in El Born, and the merchants built their mansions and palaces close to the activity and business of the port, together with a fine Gothic stock exchange (**La Llotja**) and a magnificent church, **Santa Maria del Mar**.

The best place to feel a sense of this expanding late-medieval city is in the grand Gothic mansions of Carrer de Montcada, where the **Museu Picasso** is just one of several museums and galleries to take advantage of the buildings' graceful space. Among others are the textile museum (**Museu Tèxtil i d'Indumentària**) and the adjoining **Museu Barbier-Mueller d'Art Precolombi**, with early Latin-American artefacts, and the art galleries of **Sala Montcada** and the **Galeria Maeght**. At the end of the street is the rewarding **El Xampanyet**, a delightful small bar that serves *cava*, Spain's sparkling wine.

The **Mercat del Born** was an open-air market until 1876 when it was covered over with what was then the largest iron structure in Spain, covering 17,200sq m (185,000sq ft). Recent excavations have revealed important pre-18th-century foundations. Today the area around the market is a lively nocturnal haunt, with trendy small restaurants and bars.

The dazzling MACBA, Museum of Contemporary Art

Walk: Ciutat Vella

This walk takes in the most important sites in the old town. It is easy to become sidetracked in the lanes and alleys that meander between the great buildings, but do not worry if you get lost – that is half the fun. And you will soon find a landmark to get your bearings.

Allow half a day.

Start at Urquinaona metro (line 1 & 4). Jaume I (line 4) in Via Laietana is the nearest Metro at the end of the walk.

1 Palau de la Música Catalana

There are few examples of *modernisme* in the old town and few greater *modernista* buildings than this music hall, which is a UNESCO World Heritage Site. Designed by Lluís Domènech i Montaner and completed in 1908, it has a dazzling façade of mosaics, statues and brickwork. Recent extensions by local architect Oscar Tusquets have exposed more of the magnificent details and include a gourmet restaurant. A beautiful inverted dome of coloured glass diffuses the light in the auditorium, which has sculptures of Richard Wagner and Josep Anselm Clavé, who founded the Orfeó Català choral society for which the building was created.

Carrer de Sant Francesc de Paula 2. Tel: 932 957 200. Guided tours (50 mins) every 30 mins daily 10am–3pm; July–Sept 10am–7pm. Tel: 902 442 882. www.palaumusica.org. Admission charge. Head south on V. Laietana and turn right at Av. Catedral.

2 Catedral

On the site of a Roman temple, the cathedral was begun in 1298 and not completed until the 20th century. Its oldest part is a small Romanesque chapel dedicated to Santa Lucia, though the cathedral is dedicated to Santa Eulàlia, a 4th-century martyr and the city's patron, who is entombed in the crypt. The church has a nave and 28 side chapels, with a notable painting by Bernat Martorell

The sumptuous Palau de la Música Catalana

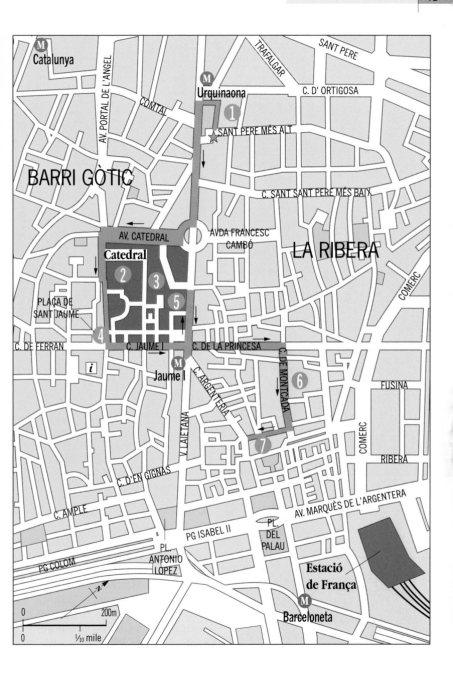

(1452) in the Capella Sant Bernat. A large plaque just to the left of the door commemorates the baptism here of Carib Indians brought back by Columbus in 1493. The cloisters are beautifully cool and keep contented geese.

Plaça de la Seu. Tel: 933 107 195. Open daily. Free.

Opposite the cathedral you'll see the Museu Frederic Marès.

3 Museu Frederic Marès

The most eclectic museum in the city was put together by the sculptor Frederic Marès (1893–1991) in part of the old Royal Palace. Religious art in the basement includes intact portals and a large collection of sculptures from around Catalonia. On the three floors above, the collection becomes more whimsical, with pipes, clocks, umbrellas and pin-up postcards.

Plaça de Sant Iu 5–6. Tel: 933 105 800. www.museumares.bcn.es. Open: Tue–Sat 10am–7pm, Sun & holidays 10am–3pm. Admission charge.

Go down to C. Jaume I and turn right to reach Plaça de Sant Jaume.

4 Plaça de Sant Jaume

The site of the Roman Forum remains the debating centre of the city. The **Casa de la Ciutat** (town hall) dates from the 14th century and its entrance is watched over by Jaume I, who granted Barcelona the right to elect its representatives, and Joan Fiveller, a fiscal hero. Its main chamber is the Saló de Cent, where the city's 100 councillors met. The Saló de les Cròniques on the first floor was decorated in 1929 by Josep-Maria Sert with murals of scenes from Catalan history.

The **Palau de la Generalitat** on the opposite side of the square is guarded by St George, patron saint of Catalonia. Seat of the Generalitat (Catalan government) since the 15th century, it has some fine interior rooms and a beautiful first-floor open patio, the Patí dels Trongers.

Both buildings are open only on specific weekends and festive days. For visits to the Town Hall tel: 934 027 364; for the Generalitat tel: 934 024 600.

Retrace your steps to C. Jaume I and turn left on V. Laietana.

5 Palau Reial Major

The royal palace of the count-kings of Barcelona is overlooked by the arcaded Torre de Martí. Beside it is the **Salò del Tinell**, a huge Gothic hall that was the

The Catedral spire watched over by gargoyles

bustling centre of the royal domain. Stairs up the tower begin in the **Capella de Santa Agata**, the royal chapel built against the Roman wall with a bell tower acting as a watchtower. The altarpiece by Jaume Huguet (1466) is the only remaining decoration in the entire royal complex. Beneath the palace you can see part of the Roman city. It can all be visited through the **Museu d'Història del la Ciutat** just off the Plaça del Rei.
Tel: 933 151 111.
www.museuhistoria.bcn.es. Open:
Tue–Sat 10am–8pm, Sun & holidays
10am–3pm. Admission charge.
Return to V. Laietana and turn right,
then left at C. de la Princesa. Turn right
at C. de Montcada.

6 Museu Picasso

The Picasso Museum is housed in five Gothic palaces in a street so narrow the roofs nearly touch. The buildings alone are worth a visit; the paintings and drawings by the city's favourite adopted son (*see pp48–9*) make it unmissable.
Carrer de Montcada 15–23. Tel: 933 196
310. www.museupicasso.bcn.es. Open:
Tue–Sun 10am–8pm. Admission charge.
Continue down C. de Montcada and turn
right into Plaça Santa Maria.

7 Església de Santa Maria del Mar

The city's finest church is a simple Gothic masterpiece raised from nothing in 1384 after just 55 years in the building. Its three lofty naves are almost identical and their octagonal columns an impressive 13m (43ft) apart. The 14th-century rose window replaced the original lost in an earth tremor. The acoustics are excellent and there are often concerts here, including jazz.
Plaçs Santa Maria. Open daily:
9.30am–1.30pm, 4.30–8pm. Free.

The entrance to the chapel of St Agatha and the heart of the Royal Palace

The Museu Picasso in Barcelona has the largest collection of the artist's works in the world. Much of it is fascinating material from his childhood and precocious art-school years. Though he lived in the city for only a short time, it left an indelible mark on him and his work, and the museum is as much his homage to the city as it is the city's to its talented son.

Pablo Picasso was born in 1881 in Málaga, where his mother, Maria Picasso, came from. His father, José Ruiz Blasco, was an art teacher from the Basque country and he was offered a job teaching in Barcelona's art school, then situated above the Llotja (stock exchange) when Pablo was nearly 14. The family eventually settled in Carrer de Mercè 3 not far from the school, which Pablo began to attend. His precocious talent flourished, and he was a highly accomplished formal painter even in his mid-teens.

At the school he made a lifetime friend in the artist Manuel Pallarès, who came from the town of Horta de Ebro. Picasso's subsequent trips to this village are recorded in pictures in the gallery. Fond of the lowlife, the two friends visited the prostitutes in Carrer d'Avinyó and their experience inspired *Les Demoiselles d'Avignon* (1906–7, Museum of Modern Art, New York), the painting considered by many historians to be the starting point of modern art.

Picasso's father rented him a studio in Calle de la Plata 4, where he executed

Contemporary Art Collection

the large canvas of a woman on her sick bed titled *Science and Charity* (197 × 249.5cm), which was sent to the General Fine Arts Exhibition in Madrid in 1897.

Setting up on his own in various studios, Picasso was a regular visitor to Els Quatre Gats, the artists' café in Carrer Montsió, where he had his first exhibition at the age of 20. In this milieu he mingled with the best of Barcelona's contemporary painters, such as Ramon Casas and Santiago Rusiñol, as well as Jaime Sabartés y Gual, a poet and writer the same age as himself, who became a good friend in Paris.

Paris was the place for artists to head for, and in 1904 Picasso set off for the city, leaving Barcelona for good. He returned sporadically, mostly to see his family, but in 1917 he did a series of paintings in the city when he visited with Diaghilev's Ballet Russe, for which he had painted the scenery.

His feelings about the Civil War were expressed in *Guernica* (Museo Reina Sofia, Madrid), his painting depicting the suffering of the people of the Basque village when it was bombed by Franco's German allies on 26 April 1937, a market day.

The Franco regime kept him in exile but it did not keep his paintings away, and from the mid-1950s the Gaspard Gallery regularly exhibited his work. On these occasions Sabartés would return to Barcelona and it was very much his influence, together with donations of Picassos from his own collection, that led the municipality to establish a museum for his friend in 1963. When Sabartés died five years later, Picasso added to the museum by donating in his memory the 58-picture series *Las Meninas*, a homage to Spain's great painter Diego Velásquez.

In 1970, three years before his death in France, Picasso made further donations of 900 paintings, drawings and other items that had been in his parents' house when he went to live in Paris.

Opposite: Els Quatre Gats café in Carrer Montsió where Picasso had his first exhibition
Above: There is no escaping Picasso!

Walk: Raval

From old buildings that formerly housed thousands of orphans to dazzling modern cultural centres, from avant-garde galleries to trendy bars, this walk in the once-neglected Raval district of the Old Town is a fine example of the fascinating diversity that characterises Barcelona.
Allow 1–2 hours.

From the top of La Rambla turn into Carrer Bonsuccés which leads into Plaça Bonsuccés. Cut through the arch into Plaça Vicenç Martorell. Some of this walk can be traced on the map of La Rambla (p87).

1 Casa de la Misericòrdia
Now used as municipal offices for the Ciutat Vella district, this building dates from 1583. It was one of many religious institutions and convents that were situated on this side of La Rambla, just outside the city wall. A testimony to its past as a hospice for abandoned children is a curious hole in the wall, through which babies were passed to merciful nuns.

2 La Central del Raval
Cut through the café of the adjoining bookshop which is in the chapel of the Casa de la Misericòrdia to get an idea of the extent of this medieval complex, and to see Barcelona 20th-century design at its best – a clever combination of ancient and modern.
Pass the books to the entrance in the street Elisabets, then right into Elisabets and right again into Montalegre.

3 Centre de Cultura Contemporània de Barcelona
Known as the CCCB, this centre for contemporary culture has a busy programme of exhibitions and diverse cultural activities. A former orphanage, it was converted into this magnificent space by architects Piñon and Vilaplana, part of the flurry of activity pre- and post-Olympics.
Carrer Montalegre 5. Tel: 933 064 100. www.cccb.org. Admission charge.

4 Museu d'Art Contemporani (MACBA)
The enormous building that houses the Contemporary Art Museum sits large and dazzling on the Plaça dels Angels. Its collection includes post-1950s Catalan and Spanish art, as well as some international pieces, and interesting temporary exhibitions (*see p135*).
From Plaça dels Angels go down Carrer dels Angels and turn left into Carrer del Carme (see map p87).

5 Antic Hospital de la Santa Creu
Often overlooked, this Gothic complex is a gem. It was used as a hospital until the 1920s, when it moved to the new Santa Creu i Sant Pau designed by

modernista Domènech i Montaner in the Eixample (*see p116*). The Institut d'Estudis Catalans with its magnificent tile work now occupies the convalescent wing. Wander through the shady courtyard perfumed by orange blossom, past the Library of Catalonia and the Massana art school until you emerge in Carrer Hospital.

Turn right into Carrer Hospital and follow it until it opens into the Rambla del Raval.

6 Rambla del Raval

This new Rambla is emblematic of the city council's policy of urban regeneration. Despite fierce criticism they went ahead and bulldozed several streets of old but occupied housing to create this bright boulevard. Bathed in bright sunlight, it contrasts sharply with the dark streets of the past.

Today local residents enjoy it as a leisure space, sitting at its terrace cafés while kids speed by on bikes and skateboards. The Filmoteca (film theatre) is being built here.

The rotund cat at the end of the Rambla is unmistakably the work of Colombian artist Botero.

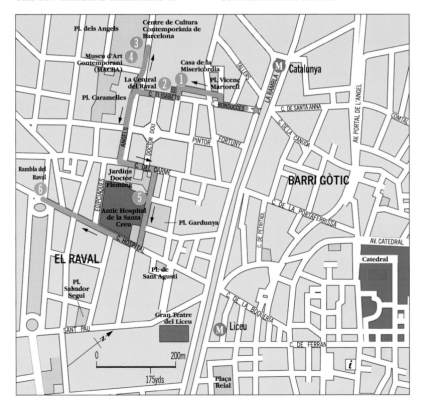

Barcelona's fortune was founded on the sea. Once a great naval power, it had a dockyard that furnished the royal fleet and rivalled those of Genoa and Venice. From here Catalans set off on their conquests of the Balearics and places further afield, and it was here that Christopher Columbus stepped ashore in triumph after his discovery of America.

Barcelona's mastery of the seas began in the reign of Jaume I, el Conqueridor (James I, 1213–76). He extended

Catalonia's territories, taking the Balearic islands of Mallorca and Ibiza from the Moors. During his reign the *Llibre de Consulat de Mar* was drawn up as a code of trading practice throughout the Mediterranean.

Catalonia had a flamboyant admiral in Roger de Llúria, scourge of the French, who killed the Provençal admiral Guíllen Corner in single combat when he jumped aboard the French ship in an encounter off Malta in 1283. More menacing was Roger de Flor, described by a contemporary as 'of terrible aspect, quick in gesture and imperious in action'. He was admiral of the fleet of King Frederick of Sicily during a French attempt to recapture the island, and he went on to command a fearful crew of Catalan and Aragonese mercenaries known as the Almogàvars.

By this time Barcelona was the wealthiest mercantile state in the Mediterranean, importing gold from north Africa and spices from the east. A century before Columbus set sail from Seville, the great Catalan poet Ramon Lull (1232–1315) wrote *Arte de Navigar*, in which he detailed methods of navigation using charts and astrolabes and making the first mention of the magnetic needle. Realising the earth was round, he foresaw the Americas – 'a continent against which the water strikes when displaced, as happens on our side, which is, in respect to the other, the eastern side'.

When Columbus returned from his second voyage in 1494, he was greeted in Barcelona by Ferdinand and Isabella. But the discovery of the New World held few benefits for Barcelona, as trade was granted exclusively to Seville and the Atlantic port of Cadiz.

By the 16th century the seas were largely at the mercy of Barbary pirates and corsairs. The northern Mediterranean states were finally galvanised into action, and trees were felled across Catalonia to build the ships that sailed from its shores to join the Venetian forces against the Ottomans. They met off the Greek coast at Lepanto, led by the flagship of Don John of Austria, which now resides in replica in Barcelona's former dockyards, the Drassanes.

Mercantile fortunes did not revive until the 19th century when Barcelona was permitted to trade with South America. Many Catalans had gone to make their fortunes in Cuba, and Habaneras, sea shanties from Havana, are still sung during festivals on the Costa Brava.

The first steam ship to go into service was the *Balear*, which had its maiden run to the Balearic Islands in 1833, and a final moment of nautical glory was achieved when *Ictíneo*, a submarine invented by Narcís Montoriol from Figueres, slipped beneath the waves in the port in 1859. A replica sits beside by Port Vell.

Opposite: Columbus points to the open sea
Above: Leisure craft in the port with the old customs house behind

Walk: Port Vell

A boat trip aboard a *Golondrina* ('swallow') around Barcelona's port puts the city into perspective. Ashore, it is pleasant to wander along the quayside of the Moll de la Fusta and Moll d'Espanya. Often there are tall ships visiting, and you can always guess at the lives of the owners of the luxury yachts in the Marina Port Vell.

Allow two hours.

The Drassanes metro station (line 3) is the nearest to the World Trade Center.

Columbus looks down on the port

1 World Trade Center
Standing at the end of the Moll de Barcelona, for all the world like one of the visiting passenger liners that draws up alongside it, the World Trade Center is an architectural showcase designed by the American firm of Pei, Cobb, Fred and Partners, who also gave us the glass pyramid outside the Louvre in Paris. There are four eight-storey buildings, three of which are for commercial use, the fourth the five-star Grand Marina Hotel. Also here is Ruccola (*tel: 935 088 268*), one of the most fashionable restaurants in the city, with top chef, Joan Piqué.

Head up Moll de Barcelona and cross Pl. de les Drassanes to reach Av. del Paral.lel.

2 Museu Marítim
One of the principal reasons for going to the maritime museum is to look at the Reials Drassanes, the royal dockyards, in which the collection of boats, charts and models is housed. It is an extraordinary piece of medieval civic architecture, a row of bays in which galleys were built, then slipped into the water (which now lies 100m or so away). There is a replica of the galley (one of the many vast vessels built here) which achieved glory at the Battle of Lepanto.

Go back to Pl. de les Drassanes and turn left on Moll de la Fusta.

3 Monument à Colom
This figure of Christopher Columbus stands in the Plaça Portal de la Pau, the landing stage for the city where the navigator, his wife, three sons, fellow sailors and seven Carib Indians stepped ashore after the triumphant discovery of the Americas. The statue was designed for the Universal Exhibition of 1888 by Gaietà Buïgas i Monravà. A lift takes visitors to a viewing platform near the top of the 60m (200ft) column, which was made in part from melted-down cannon from the castle on Montjuïc.

Open: 9am–8.30pm. Admission charge. The Port Authority building is across the road.

4 Junta d'Obres del Port

The Port Authority building was the reception point for passengers after it was built in 1907 by the engineer Julio Valdés.

Continue on Moll de la Fusta and turn right on Moll d'Espanya.

5 Moll d'Espanya

The main arm extending into Port Vell houses two yacht clubs and a variety of leisure facilities, including a number of restaurants, bars and elegant shops situated in the **Maremàgnum** mall. There is an IMAX **cinema** and a walk-through **aquarium**, the largest in Europe, where you can surround yourself with sharks, rays and many other species of fish.

Tel: 932 217 474. Open: 9.30am–9pm, July–Aug 9.30am–11pm. Admission charge.
Go back up to Moll de la Fusta, turn right, and continue around the marina to Passeig Borbó.

6 Museu d'Història de Catalunya

The museum of the history of Catalonia is sited in the Palau de Mar, the sole surviving warehouses on the Moll de Barceloneta, built by Elies Rogent. The handsome, honey-coloured brick building has restaurants with tables on the Marina Port Vell quayside. The view from the café on the top storey alone is worth the admission charge (*see p135*).

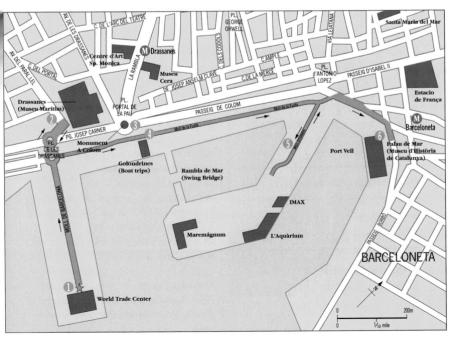

Diagonal

This arterial road that cuts diagonally across the city is one of the most distinctive avenues in Barcelona. Despite the density of its traffic, broad tree-shaded pavements and notable architecture lend it a certain elegance. Whether you take the recently inaugurated tram, or whizz down in the open-air tourist bus, it's worth getting a glimpse of this angle on Barcelona.

The changing face of the Diagonal

What's in a name?
The name Diagonal is loaded with connotations. Like many places in Barcelona, this street proudly reverted to its Catalan Avinguda Diagonal in 1979, shedding the Castilian Avenida del Generalísimo Franco which had been imposed in 1939 after the dictator's victory in the Civil War. Today the name has taken on a new significance because of its associations with the Diagonal Mar, the thrusting new residential area of Barcelona where the Forum 2004 took place.

From the top
The cars that flood in to the city every morning along the upper reaches of the Diagonal – from the dormitory towns along the industrial River Llobregat – pass luxury hotels, exclusive residential blocks, a university campus, rank upon rank of office blocks and even a royal palace and a polo club. This is a world apart from the dark, narrow alleyways of the Gothic quarter, or the bustling commerce of the Eixample. Each building is its own island, like the people working or living within them. There is none of the intimate jostle you get in the bars and markets downtown.

Changing gear
After Plaça Francesc Macià the façades of the elegant 19th-century buildings are warmer, with fine shops at street level

The Catalan work ethic is reflected in the abundance of banks

A tram on Diagonal

by the sea, passing the latest landmarks like the Jean Nouvel Torre Agbar in the Plaça de les Glòries, and the new technology district 22@.

Diagonal Mar Park showing work in progress

and some key examples of *modernista* architecture. Between Passeig de Gràcia and Pau Claris is the Palau Baró de Quadras, beautifully restored to become the Casa Asia and well worth visiting (*Av Diagonal 373. Open: Mon–Sat 10am–8pm, Sun 10am–2pm. Free admission*). Further on is the Casa Terrades, designed by the same architect Puig i Cadafalch, popularly known as Casa de les Punxes, for its fairy-tale spires.

New horizons

The last stretch of this long straight avenue is the latest to be developed. Slicing through the former industrial district of Poble Nou, it leads into Barcelona's brand-new residential area

ABOVE THE DIAGONAL

The expression 'above the Diagonal' is loaded with ironic social connotations: those who live on the mountain side of the avenue reputedly regard themselves as a cut above those who live beneath it. It is a dangerous generalisation, though it is true to say that the smarter residential areas, more expensive restaurants and boutiques tend to be above this imaginary dividing line and many of its older residents only venture into the old town when it is opera night at the Liceu. They are part of an urban tribe known as *pijos/pijas* who congregate in the smarter cafeterias like Sandor in Plaça Francesc Macià, a strategic roundabout which marks the point where the modern stretch of Diagonal meets the part that cuts through the blocks of the Eixample.

The organisation of large-scale events has become a tradition in Barcelona's history. The whole world heard about the success of the 1992 Olympics, and while the 1888 and 1929 Universal Exhibitions made less impact internationally they certainly left their stamp on the city. The most recent venture was the Forum 2004, a first in world history.

No one quite knows how the idea for a Universal Forum of Cultures was first conceived. Rumour has it that during the 1992 Olympics the charismatic former mayor Pasqual Maragall astounded his colleagues by suddenly announcing it as the next major event, a new goal for the city to work towards.

Jointly organised by the City Council, the Generalitat of Catalonia and the Spanish government, and with the backing of all 186 member countries of UNESCO, the long expensive preparations were heavily criticised but nevertheless the project forged ahead. From May to September 2004 major exhibitions, festivals, theatre, music, dance, cabaret, circuses and puppet shows took place in the Forum venue in Diagonal Mar and all around the city.

The main themes were worthy: cultural diversity, sustainable development and conditions for peace. Considered the key issues facing the world in the 21st century, these became the core themes for all the activities, particularly the regular debates and conferences led by such figures as Mikhail Gorbachev, most of which were open to the public.

Behind these high ideals there was an inevitable subtext, and in keeping with the '92 Olympics Barcelona will benefit from the Forum's legacy. The huge investments have resulted in a brand-new residential area, Diagonal Mar, which consists of high-rise homes with a sea view, several seaside hotels, a park designed by the late Enric Miralles, prestigious Catalan architect, and the

inevitable shopping centre. The Forum was another opportunity for world-class architects to include a piece in the architectural showcase that Barcelona has become. The main Forum building was designed by Swiss architects Herzog and De Meuron.

This is new Barcelona, created largely by property developers and heavyweight investors. The legacy includes an enormous conference centre and thousands of square metres of office space. However, it also has its popular side. The people of Barcelona have inherited a new leisure area. By the summer of 2005 local residents of this once marginalised area were swimming in the Forum's saltwater lake and soon there will be a huge marina offering watersports to all, as well as a maritime zoo.

Below: Modern architecture at the Forum

Eixample

One striking feature of any map of Barcelona is that the majority of its blocks of buildings have their corners knocked off. This is the unique style of the Eixample (the expansion), the 19th-century development that spread dramatically out of the old town and became the springboard for the new architecture – *modernisme*.

Modernista pharmacy

The industrial revolution attracted huge numbers of immigrants to Barcelona in the 19th century, and it soon became clear that not just a few suburbs were needed to cope with this increased population, but a whole new city had to be built. Leaving the old town to its own devices, the city was to extend to fill the plain between the hills of Tibidabo and Montjuïc, and between the Llobregat and Besòs rivers.

Ildefons Cerdà

When architects were invited to submit plans for the new city the town hall chose one drawn up by its own architect, Antoni Rovira i Trias, which envisaged roads radiating out like spokes from the old city. However, the decision was reversed by the authorities in Madrid, who for reasons that were never made clear insisted on another design: one submitted by Ildefons Cerdà i Sunyer (1815–76), a utopian civil engineer and parliamentary deputy who had a walrus moustache and a record of collecting statistical material about the state of the city. His plans, which can be seen in the Museu d'Història de la Ciutat, consisted of row upon row of square grids measuring 133m by 133m

(436ft by 436ft) with streets 20m wide. Buildings would occupy two sides of each 'island', allowing for extensive gardens and parks, and the whole area would be crossed by three major avenues, two running diagonally, meeting at Plaça de les Glòries. There would be a total of 550 blocks with angled corners (*xamfrans*), patios and gardens, and everyone would live in harmony: there would be no rich or poor end of town.

Speculators step in

That was the ideal, and in 1860 the first stone of this great plan was laid by Isabella II and the streets given the names of all the heroes in Catalonia's history. But it was more than a decade before the city's economy was in good enough shape for building work really to get under way. When it did start, it happened piecemeal, much of it falling to speculators and unscrupulous landlords. Cerdà's plans were ignored and the parks and green areas built over – except for the Parc de l'Escorxador, now the Parc Joan Miró, signposted by the sculptor's colourful 22m (70ft) *Dona i Ocell* (*Woman and Bird*).

Little by little, however, money came

in and allowed for grander houses to be designed. Market forces also came into play to make the area around Passeig de Gràcia and the right side of the new railway running inland from Plaça Catalunya more desirable than the land on the left side of the tracks. It was on the left side that the first major public building in the Eixample was constructed in 1872 – the university,

designed by Elies Rogent i Amat. The right side, the *dreta*, was where the showcase houses were built. The height limitation on buildings was raised.

The Quadrat d'Or

The generation of architects who came after Cerdà were not imbued with the same utopian socialism, and many of them saw the grids of the original plan as a constraint on human endeavour. By the time they were on the scene in the 1890s they began to pull down some of the first buildings to create bigger and better homes, particularly around the Passeig de Gràcia, creating a 'Quadrat d'Or', a golden square of *modernista* excellence. Bordered by Plaça Catalunya, Carrer de Aribau, Avinguda de Diagonal and Passeig Saint Joan, this area of around 100 blocks has the highest concentration of *modernista* buildings in the city, with works by most of its great practitioners. Among them is the former publishing house Editorial Montaner i Simon in Carrer d'Aragó. Designed by the owner's brother,

Fundació Antoní Tàpies in the Quadrat d'Or, by Domènech i Montaner

Lluís Domènech i Montaner, in 1879, it was the first private buiding in the city to use an ironwork structure. It is now a gallery for Catalonia's best-known contemporary artist, Antoni Tàpies (*see p134*). Some are now commercial premises, housing offices and smart shops, but many remain as apartment blocks.

The last chapter

Cerdà's plans, which had such an impact on the city, have adapted and mellowed over the years, depending on taste, need and city fortunes. The story ends with Forum 2004 (*see pp58–9*) when the Diagonal finally does Cerdà's bidding and reaches all the way down to the sea.

BENEATH THE STREETS

Cerdà's plans for the city were based on an ideal of giving the people of Barcelona better housing, and that included better health and sanitation. The first Sanitation Plan was completed by the engineer Pere Garcia Faria in 1891, and it can be seen in the Eixample's **Museu del Clavegueram** (Sewage Museum – *Passeig Sant Joan 98. Tel: 934 576 550 for an appointment for a tour of the city sewers*). The museum covers 900sq m (9,700sq ft) and looks at the city's essential waterworks from Roman times to the large-scale works carried out for the Olympic Games of 1992.

Two of the famous trio of *modernista* buildings in Passeig de Gràcia, by Puig i Cadafalch (left) and Gaudí

Joan Miró's *Woman and Bird* in The Parc de l'Escorxador, once the site of slaughterhouses

Barcelona's unique gift to architecture is a style it developed over successive generations of architects who shaped the city from around 1880 to 1930. It has its counterparts in the English Arts and Crafts movement, in French Art Nouveau and in German Jugendstil. But it also had its own inspiration in Catalan Gothic and the *mudéjar* style of Islam.

When the city broke down its medieval walls and took up the plans for an extension (Eixample, *see pp60–63*), there was plenty of room for creativity and development. But it was not until the Universal Exhibition of 1888 that a new local style could be detected. The exhibition was held in the recently landscaped Parc de la Ciutadella (*see pp102–3*). A keynote was set by Josep Vilaseca's Arc de Triomf, but of greater impact was the work of a popular 38-year-old professor from Barcelona

University's School of Architecture, Lluís Domènech i Montaner. For visitors to the exhibition he designed the Gran Hotel Internacional to cater for 1,000 guests, and had it built by the port in just 53 days. Nobody could ignore such panache.

For the exhibition he designed the Café-Restaurant based on the medieval stock exchange in Valencia. With intricate brick and ironwork, it was dismissed by many critics as backward-looking, but the architect wanted to find local influences for the modern buildings and in so doing he begun what was later seen as the *nova scuola catalana*. After the exhibition closed, Domènech used the northeast tower of the building (now the Museu Zoològic) as a workshop to develop ironwork, ceramic tiles, stained glass and stone carving, all of which played an immensely important part in the movement that followed.

Domènech's further contributions to the city included the dazzling Palau de la Música Catalana (*see p44*) and the monumental Hospital de la Santa Creu i de Sant Pau, both exquisite examples of *modernisme*. His most successful pupil was Josep Puig i Cadafalch, who was just 15 years old when he gazed in awe at the giant hotel rising on the waterfront. Leading light of the succeeding generation of *modernista* architects, his designs were more conservative, but they included Plaça Catalunya and the 1929 Universal Exhibition in Montjuïc.

Both Domènech and Puig were also active political figures. *Modernista* design was tied to a rising sense of nationalism, of wanting something that was particularly Catalan. The Renaixença, a renaissance of Catalonia, was in full spate. There was money from South America and the industrial revolution to create patrons such as Eusebi Güell, and *modernista* architecture was applied to many commercial and industrial buildings.

Modernisme is not an easy term to attach to the variety of styles that were created during these few decades. Certainly Gaudí did not want to be associated with such liberal frivolity, and it blends into *noucentisme*, the style that followed it. But the three architects' neighbouring works in Passeig de Gràcia – Domènech's Casa Lléo Morera, Puig's Casa Amatller and Gaudí's Casa Batlló (*see p68*) – show just how different and exciting the times were in which they lived.

Opposite: Casa Milà
Above: Coloured ceramic mosaics were an integral part of *modernista* houses

Walk: Passeig de Gràcia and Rambla Catalunya

The only way to appreciate *modernista* architecture fully is to wander around the streets of the Eixample, looking up at roof details, spotting decorative balconies, pausing in doorways to admire the tiling or some elaborate staircase. This walk up and down the two main streets of the district allows you to do just that, taking in some of the key buildings of that era, as well as getting the feel of the elegant heart of contemporary Barcelona.

Allow 1–2 hours (not including pauses for coffee, visits to buildings or shopping, all of which you will be tempted to do).

From Plaça Catalunya walk up Passeig de Gràcia and cross Gran Via.

1 J Roca

This jewellery shop was designed in 1934 by a young Josep Lluís Sert, close friend of artist Joan Miró. It is one of the few pieces he built in Barcelona before going into exile in the USA after the Civil War. He designed the Spanish Republican

La Pedrera, Gaudí's revolutionary apartment block

Pavilion for the 1937 Paris International Exhibition where Picasso's *Guernica* was first exhibited and after Franco's death returned to build the magnificent Miró Foundation on Montjuïc.

A little further north of J Roca you'll find the lampposts.

2 Lamppost

A trademark of Passeig de Gràcia, these wrought-iron lampposts designed by municipal architect Pere Falqués in 1906 must be some of the most beautiful in the world, and some of the few you can sit under. They can be spotted all the way up this handsome avenue which once joined Barcelona to the former village of Gràcia. Notice the Gaudí hexagonal pavement tiles, which are now for sale in smart souvenir shops. *Continue up Passeig de Gràcia, crossing Diputació and Consell de Cent.*

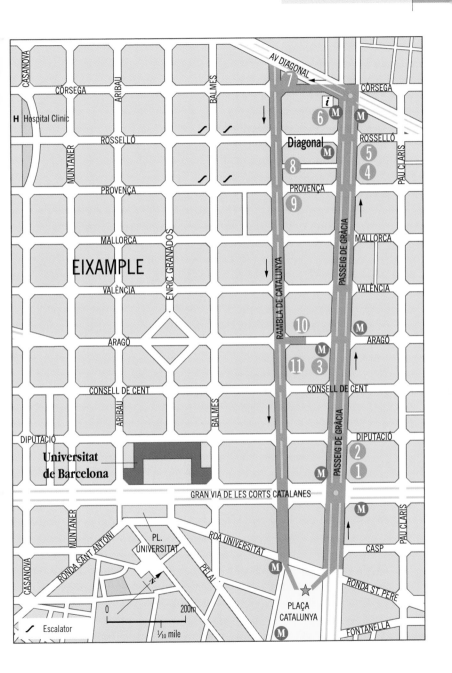

Bird's-eye view of Passeig de Gràcia

3 Illa de la Discòrdia

Cross over Consell de Cent, a street full of art galleries and fashion, and you arrive at the Casa Lleó Morera (*No 35*), the first in this block known as the 'Block of Discord' because of its discordant styles of architecture. The three main houses are by the key architects of the period. The first is the work of Domènech i Montaner, showing his decorative detailing in the wonderful ceramic work in the entrance hall. Further up at No 41 is the Casa Amatller by Puig i Cadafalch with his distinctive neo-Gothic style, and a centre for the *Ruta del Modernisme* (a do-it-yourself guided tour of *modernisme* in the city). And next door is the unmistakable hand of Gaudí in the Casa Batlló with its dream-like façade and flowing interior. The house is now open to the public, an opportunity that should not be missed. *Tel: 932 160 306. www.casabatllo.es. Open: daily 9am–8pm. Admission charge. Carry on up Passeig de Gràcia until you reach the junction with Provença.*

4 Casa Milà

Further up the street is the Casa Milà,

one of Gaudí's most famous buildings. Popularly known as La Pedrera (the Quarry) for its roughly honed façade, this apartment block was built in 1910. It is worth visiting for a deeper insight into Gaudí, for its spectacular roof terrace, for *El Pis*, a show flat decorated as a period piece, and for the sheer beauty of it. Owned and maintained by local bank the Caixa de Catalunya, its exhibition space on the first floor has a programme of quality art exhibitions. *Open: daily 10am–8pm. Admission charge. The next stop is just before Rosselló.*

5 Casa de Ramon Casas

The house at No 96 was the home and studio of *modernista* painter Ramon Casas. His work can be seen in the Museu MNAC (*see p136*). Today it is the home of Vinçon, selling everything from corkscrews to couches, a mecca for the design-conscious. Slip into the patio from its first floor for a glimpse of Casas' studio and to get an idea of the typical patio of the Eixample blocks. *Cross Rosselló and Palau Robert is on the left-hand side.*

6 Palau Robert

Across the road, just before Avinguda Diagonal, is the Tourist Information Centre for Catalonia. The shady gardens behind are peaceful and a pleasant short cut through to Còrsega and on to Rambla de Catalunya. *Continue up to Av Diagonal, then turn left on Còrsega.*

7 Casa Serra

The original house built by Puig i Cadafalch in 1908 was adapted to accommodate the Diputació de Barcelona, the body representing Spain's central government, in the 1980s with an ingenious modern extension by influential Olympic architects Milà and Correa. From here the elegant length of Rambla Catalunya stretches down to Plaça Catalunya. Since the mid-19th century it has been the classic avenue for strolling down, pausing for a refreshing *orxata* and people-watching. This is the place to spot the bourgeois Catalans, immaculately coiffed and dressed, walking their dogs or grandchildren and meeting friends.

Turn left and head south on Rambla de Catalunya, crossing over Rosselló again.

8 Passatge de la Concepció

One of several passageways with pretty terraced houses and sometimes gardens *a la inglesa* that cut through the typical Eixample block. Passatge Permanyer between Pau Claris and Roger de Llúria is another attractive example. Somewhat exclusive as homes, this one is known for its trendy and stylish 'sister' restaurants, Tragaluz and El Japonés, and leads back to Passeig de Gràcia.

Continue south, crossing Provença.

9 Maurí

On the crossroads with Provença are two flagship Catalan establishments. Maurí is a desirable pastry shop and delicatessen, where silver-haired ladies meet for lunch or *berenar* (an afternoon snack). On the opposite *xamfran* (corner) is Groc, the original Toni Miró shop, wonderfully low-key for the birthplace of an empire.

Carry on down Rambla de Catalunya until the junction with Aragó.

10 Fundació Tàpies

Cross Aragó and look back at the Tàpies Foundation for a better appreciation of this building. Its temporary exhibitions are high-quality. Housed in a former publishing firm designed by Domènech i Montaner, it is crowned by an original Tàpies sculpture *Núvol i Cadira* (*Cloud and Chair*).

Open: Tue–Sun 10am–8pm. See p134. Cross Aragó.

11 Galeria Joan Prats

Just below Aragó on the left is one of the city's oldest and most famous art galleries, Joan Prats, known for its exhibitions of leading contemporary art. Its beautiful painted glass frontage is just one of many on Rambla Catalunya. On the other side of the road is the Casa Miquel Fargas, a suitably decorative setting for Muxart, the shoe shop. Designed by Catalan Hermenegildo Muxart, these wildly creative shoes are works of art.

Continue down Rambla Catalunya until it meets Plaça Catalunya, after which it becomes La Rambla. Alternatively, take Consell de Cent and head back to Passeig de Gràcia and the metro.

The impressive chimneys on the roof of Casa Milà

These two words have been irrevocably linked since the surge of activity in the 1980s, when pent-up creative energy was unleashed with the return of democracy in Spain. In Catalonia it was fuelled by the Olympic Games in 1992 but the momentum continues in the 21st century: 2003 was the Year of Design in Barcelona and a Design Museum is to be built in Glòries.

But this is hardly a new phenomenon. There is an undeniable creative streak running through Catalan blood. Gaudí was not just a genius but wildly creative. And look at the industrialist Güell who was daring enough to be his patron. The whole *modernista* movement depended on the support of the Catalan bourgeoisie. Catalans are not afraid to stand out of line – in fact they are delighted to be different from the more conservative Madrid. They also have an innate sense of style – in their dress, homes and offices, designer labels are the thing. Hence the success of establishments like Vinçon, a design emporium on Passeig de Gràcia which manages to sell a table mat as a designer item. Nearby is another interiors shop, possibly the most beautiful in Barcelona, BD Ediciones de Diseño (*Mallorca 291*). Selling the best of 20th-century design, its own interior won an award in 1979 for its renovation, within Domènech i Montaner's Casa Thomas.

The boom time in the 1980s saw the opening of the famous designer bars,

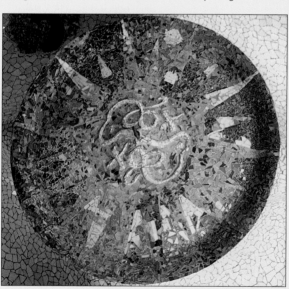

most of which are still open: Nick Havanna (*Rosselló 208*), Universal (*Marià Cubí 184*), Otto Zutz, the designer disco (*Lincoln 15*), Zsa Zsa (*Rosselló 156*). At the same time Barcelona became the centre of the fashion industry in Spain, led by Antonio Miró who remains supreme. Younger designers like Josep Font, Josep Abril and David Valls have also made an impact on the international scene. And in the world of advertising Barcelona agencies regularly bring home the top creative awards from international festivals.

Just as the establishment had sponsored the *modernista* architects at the start of the 20th century, and the new Eixample was a showcase of Barcelona's creativity, so did the authorities encourage the design movement in the aftermath of Franco. It became an integral part of their ambitious plans for the city. Dynamic mayor Pasqual Maragall and his city council were instrumental in the dramatic changes to Barcelona, using the Olympic Games as a catalyst to execute long-overdue projects for the city which, as the promotional campaigns said at the time, would benefit the citizens of Barcelona in the future. Even the Games were 'Designer Olympics', from the Toni Miró uniforms to Javier Mariscal's mascot 'Cobi'. Sculptures by national and international artists appeared in newly created squares and parks that opened up dense inner-city districts. A new airport was built by Ricardo Bofill, complete with designer palm trees. Designer Barcelona was on display in 1992 for millions of visitors. The resulting boom in tourism and business has provoked more designer activity. Visitors now stay in boutique hotels, shop in designer markets and dine on designer tapas. The trend continues.

Opposite: A Gaudí mosaic panel from Park Güell
Below: Rear view of Cobi, the first designer Olympic mascot

Gràcia

Slightly off the tourist track, the city district of Gràcia and its socially cohesive community offers a real slice of atmospheric Mediterranean life. So far untouched by major development projects, it is also home to a delightful early building by Gaudí.

Plaça Rius i Taulet

Stretching up to the Park Güell above the Diagonal, Gràcia was formerly a town in its own right (it was annexed by Barcelona in 1897) and has always kept its distinctive identity and personality. Residents are proud to be *Graciencs* first and Barcelonans second. Many of Gràcia's place names, like Carrer de la Fraternitat, Plaça de la Revolució and Mercat de la Llibertat, bear witness to the town's reputation as a centre of radical activity, while recent additions to the people's-hero tradition are squares named after John Lennon and Anne Frank.

Gràcia Village begins at the top of Passeig de Gràcia

The neighbourhood is a crisscross of narrow streets studded with tree-shaded squares that serve as social centres, perfect for lounging on café terraces and people-watching: you may well see locals in dressing gowns and slippers popping out for a loaf of freshly baked bread or the morning paper. Still a bastion of artisans and small family businesses, Gràcia has a well-integrated gypsy community and its cheap old premises are a haven for the New Age movement.

Time warp

In sightseeing terms, the highlight of Gràcia is the surprising Casa Vicens, Gaudí's early Moorish-style building tucked away unpretentiously in the narrowest of streets. While the main shopping streets like Gran de Gràcia, Travessera de Gràcia and Torrent de l'Olla are busy day and night, many of the side streets are pedestrianised and peaceful. Old-fashioned shops in dark cluttered premises rub shoulders with big-name franchises, designer boutiques with junk shops, alternative therapy centres with gaudy bargain bazaars. Here locals queue around the block for dried chickpeas and lentils, spit-roasted chickens and cut-price underwear. Unique establishments suspended in a blissful time warp before Barcelona's obsession with retail design are still to be found, like the Ferreteria Soriano at Gran de Gràcia 53, with its antiquated display windows jammed with every kitchen utensil the human mind could conceive of.

Vibrant

The long Carrer Verdi is one of the hubs of Gràcia's vibrant cultural scene and nightlife, attracting people from all over Barcelona. Activities include social events and handicrafts workshops, alternative and mainstream theatre, cinemas showing subtitled (not dubbed) films, clubs and bars, and eateries serving everything from the rustic Catalan tomato-scraped doorsteps of bread with ham and sausages to first-class seafood, pizzas and late-night Moroccan and Lebanese dishes.

Summer festival

Creative imagination is something that Gràcia shares with Gaudí. The summer extravaganza, the *festa major* or annual town festival, in mid-August draws thousands from across the city.

Residents' committees spend the best part of the year drawing up and executing their plans for the Best Street competition, for which entire streets are transformed into themed settings: science fiction worlds, medieval towns, Jurassic parks, Moorish gardens… Each group of streets organises its own nonstop programme of entertainments such as chess and dominoes tournaments, children's chocolate parties and puppet shows, foam machines and street discos.

Stages are set up in the squares for dancing to live salsa and rock late into the night.

Gràcia is characterised by small squares, many of which have been renovated and landscaped

Walk: Gràcia

Gràcia was formerly a thriving town, and was annexed to Barcelona in 1897. Quiet narrow streets and big shady squares form the fabric of what is one of the city's most dynamic and popular neighbourhoods.

Allow 2–3 hours including browsing and stops for rest and refreshment.

The walk begins at Fontana metro station on Gràcia's main street, reached by metro line 3 or the 22, 24 or 28 bus.

Head west on Breton Herreros, then turn right and go towards Les Carolines.

1 Casa Vicens

The street is so narrow that it is impossible to get a panoramic view of this colourful turreted little castle (1883–8), the only house designed by Gaudí to have been lived in by generations of the original family without a break until the present day (not open to visitors). Gaudí's first work, it was recently nominated a World Heritage building by UNESCO.

Les Carolines 18–24.

Turn right on Les Carolines, cross Gran de Gracia and continue along Santa Agata. Go right on Badia, and right again on Asturies. Turn left on Sant Antoni.

2 Plaça Ana Frank

Renovated in 2001, this small square is graced with a statue of Anne Frank lying pensively, diary in hands, face-down on the projecting roof of the Gràcia Crafts and Civic Centre. The mosaic on the wall behind it is by the Escola Massana, Barcelona's school of art and design. The square now seems to be more of a monument to spray-paint urban art than to anything else.

Continue down Sant Antoni, crossing Montseny. Turn left on Ros de Olano and right towards Plaça del Sol.

3 Plaça del Sol

Rebuilt in the 1990s to accommodate an underground car park, this square is one of Gràcia's nerve centres, in particular frequented by young people at night. Shade from ancient overhanging trees is a boon in the hot summer. Gràcia still preserves some rather beautiful old buildings like the one on the corner of Carrer Virtut (the excellent Envalira restaurant is on the ground floor) with façade in green and white *esgrafiat*, a form of decoration very typical of Catalunya.

From the square, head south on Mariana Pineda.

4 Plaça Rius i Taulet

Down across the Travessera, one of the main commercial arteries, is Gràcia's main square, with its original Town Hall (now the Municipal District Headquarters) at the bottom end. The clock tower was built in 1864. This is where Barcelona officially (on TV) sees in the New Year. The café terraces are perfect for resting and people-watching.

Turn left on Diluvi, left again on Torrent de l'Olla, right on Penedès and left on C Mare de Deu dels Desemperats.

5 Plaça de la Revolució de Septembre de 1868

Several narrow streets take you across Torrent de l'Olla, a busy shopping street, past Gràcia's main market and back up to a square which is really a place of passage, although benches under trees afford rest. The green façade of No 24, at the bottom end, is a good example of the *esgrafiat* style. The square is the gateway to the popular Carrer Verdi, a pedestrianised street packed with ethnic shops and restaurants. The building at the corner of Carrer Vallfogona is particularly quirky and ornate.

Continue north and turn right on C de l'Or.

6 Plaça de la Virreina

Bustling Verdi leads, via the Carrer de l'Or, to this peaceful square with the plain, soothing façade of the church of Sant Joan de Gràcia. From here you can pop along the Carrer Asturies, this section of which is a cool tunnel of leafy trees, to the emblematic Plaça del Diamant, the setting of the best-known Catalan novel of the same name (*see p25*).

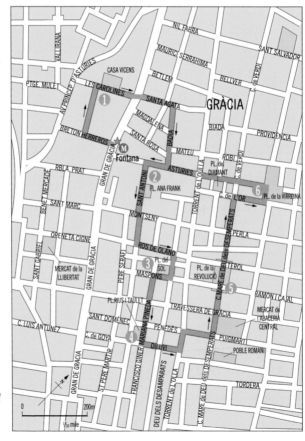

The fame of Barcelona by night has spread far and wide, not without due cause. As a result it has unfortunately become a top venue for stag nights amongst northern Europeans – who have not grasped how the locals do nightlife, gliding through with no apparent sign of intoxication and amazingly able to appear at work early the next morning.

The *Madrileños* may argue that Barcelona is tame compared with a night out in the capital city, but for most of us it is quite wild. The first important thing to understand is that nothing really gets going until after 1am. The early evening is just preamble. Whether you begin with a chilled wine in a Gothic square, a cool beer in the bustling Plaça del Sol in Gràcia, or a tapa in one of the many Basque theme bars to have opened recently, the choice is wide before dinner – which does not happen until after 9pm.

The evening can turn into night in the after-dinner bars which remain open until 2 or 3am. End the evening now and you can get a comparatively early night. It is difficult, though, to resist the temptation to go on, especially on summer nights when the night cool is the best time to be on the streets, as most of Barcelona seems to be. Around this time the clubs and discos start to get into gear. Long-standing discos

like Otto Zutz (*Lincoln 15*) or the small Club Dot (*Nou de Sant Francesc 7*) are still good value, but are being outshone by venues which often have live music earlier in the evening then metamorphose into clubs with a DJ after 2 or 3am. Most popular are the Sala Apolo (*Nou de la Rambla 113*), Cibeles (*Córsega 363*) and the eternal La Paloma (*Tigre 27*), a turn-of-the-century dance hall dripping in gilt and red velvet banquettes. Razzmatazz (*Pamplona 88*) has a lively concert and DJ programme in its three different spaces all within an old warehouse in Poble Nou. A favourite spot in the summer is the club scene on the beach near the Vila Olímpica (*Passeig Marítim*).

Some of the annual festivals feature special programming in the night, like Sonar for Advanced Music, every June, and the popular fiestas of the different *barris*, notably in Gràcia in mid-August and the main Barcelona fiesta of La Mercè in September when concerts in the squares of the Old Town may not begin until midnight. The Grec Summer Festival where most shows begin at 10pm now has an After-Grec with performances beginning after the main programming ends. There is only one solution – try a siesta.

Opposite: One of La Paloma's late-night DJ sessions
Above: A multi-space club for concerts and dance

Plaça Catalunya and La Rambla

Many towns and cities in Spain have a *rambla*, a tree-lined avenue where a stream or river once seasonally flowed. But none is as well known or as entertaining as La Rambla in Barcelona. Running from Plaça Catalunya to the port, the city's most famous highway is a slice of history and a place of continual diversions.

Miró pavement, La Rambla

Monument to Macià, much-loved President of the Generalitat in the 1930s

Plaça Catalunya

La Rambla begins at Plaça Catalunya, where the old town meets the new. Beneath this broad square, laid out in 1927, is a major railway station, a metro station and a central information point. The square is a gathering place for demonstrations and a focus of events on La Diada, Catalonia's national day (11 September). Near the metro exit is a contemporary sculpture of Francesc Macià, who boldly declared Catalonia independent shortly before the Civil War. The work is by Josep Maria Subirachs, who sculpted the angular figures on the Passion façade of the Sagrada Família.

The best-known of the many commercial premises that surround the square is **El Corte Inglés** department store, which has a fifth-floor restaurant with good views over the city.

On the southwest corner of the square is the **Café Zurich**, a historic café which, like a number of places in the Rambla, figures in *Homage to Catalonia*, George Orwell's classic story of the Civil War. It was built in 1927 as the railway's café and became a haunt of writers and chess players. During a recent major overhaul of this corner facing the Rambla it was rebuilt, but its interior remains authentic and it makes a good meeting spot.

La Rambla

Theoretically there is not one but five Ramblas (Les Rambles in Catalan, Las Ramblas in Castilian – but the singular, La Rambla, works in both languages). Today there is still a distinct flavour to each of these five sections that make up the street.

The river, the Cagallel, which had its source in the Collserola hills and dried up in summer, was converted into an underground sewer in the 14th century, by which time the city walls ran its

View of Plaça Catalunya from El Corte Inglés

whole length, on the northern (Ciutat Vella) side. From the 16th century a number of large convents were built on the opposite side of the street, giving their names to the **Rambla Santa**

Flower stalls, beautifully arranged and popular with Barcelonans, are a great attraction of La Rambla

Mònica, **Rambla St Josep** and **Rambla dels Capoutxins**, and resulting in the street being nicknamed 'Via Conventa'.

Grand houses and hotels

In the late 18th century Jaume I's city walls began to be pulled down, and the Rambla was straightened into an avenue. Large mansions such as the **Palau de la Virreina, Palau Moja** and **Casa March de Reus** were built to show off their owners' wealth. More dramatically, in 1835, Sant Josep and a college of Barefoot Trinitarians were among several religious houses burned one night by a dissatisfied mob after a disappointing bullfight, leaving space for **La Boqueria** covered market and the **Liceu** opera house to be built. Other monastic buildings were put out of use when four-fifths of the city's church land was sold off under government decree later the same year. Monastic traces can be seen in several buildings in the street, notably the **Oriente, Sant Agustí** and **Peninsular hotels** and in the **Centre d'Art Santa Mònica**.

Twenty years after the *desamortació* of

At the kiosks you will find newspapers, books, maps and postcards

the religious houses, all the fortifications had been torn down, opening up the Rambla to the old town. Plane trees were introduced, gas lighting installed and the Rambla became one of the most talked-about thoroughfares in Europe.

Famous visitors

The fame of the thoroughfare began to spread. George Sand wrote of 'coquettish' women with their tremulous fans, and men who seemed unconcerned about anything that happened outside the city. It certainly was always a place for night owls. Staying on the Rambla a century later, Rose Macaulay complained that she was woken at four in the morning by loud conversation. In *Fabled Shore* (1949), she wrote, 'Going out on my balcony and looking down I perceived that the Rambla was still full of people sitting at café tables or on seats beneath trees, or strolling to and fro, talking, laughing and screaming with the greatest vivacity, the street lights that gleamed above the plane trees now paling a little in the dawn.'

Today the Rambla extends down into the old port with an added **Rambla del Mar** bridging the water to the Moll d'Espanya. The seediness of the waterfront has disappeared, and the whole street is always a pleasant place to stroll.

Having your picture drawn is one of many ways of being diverted along the Rambla

On certain evenings from September to June an unfamiliar ripple runs down La Rambla around 8pm. There is an expensive smell in the air, and more than the usual number of men in suits and fur-coated ladies can be spotted emerging out of the metro. Silver-grey saloon cars with tinted windows queue to get into car parks. There is no mistaking the signs – it is opera night at the Gran Teatre del Liceu.

Bastion of the Catalan bourgeoisie, this opera house on La Rambla has had a variegated history since its bizarre origins in the 1830s as an amateur operatic group known as the Liceo Filodramático de Montesión whose purpose was to raise funds for a battalion of soldiers. They used to perform in an abandoned convent, the Montsió, until, flushed with success and evolving into a purely artistic group, they needed more space. In 1847 a grand new opera house on the scale of Milan's La Scala was inaugurated on the site of another former convent on La Rambla. In other European cities the opera was often sponsored by the monarchy, but the Liceu was funded by rich Catalan industrialists, and boxes were sold for life to the affluent families of Barcelona. Its first opera was Donizetti's *Anna Bolena*, but at that time performances included dance, concerts, musical comedies, plays and magic shows.

The first dramatic event in its turbulent history was in 1861 when fire destroyed the stage and auditorium, but phoenix-like it quickly reopened in 1862. Then followed a period of growth during which the distinctive divisions of Catalan society were clearly seen in the theatre's layout: the stalls and boxes were the domain of the elegantly dressed bourgeoisie while the higher seats and the gods were crammed with the lower echelons, who could barely see the stage. However, it was a time of social and political unrest and this apparent peaceful cohabitation was shaken when an anarchist threw a bomb into the stalls on the opening night of the season in 1893, killing about 20 people.

The latest dramatic incident was in 1994 when a blaze leapt out of the Liceu's roof on a January morning to the amazement of passers-by. Apparently caused by a welder's spark, it quickly took hold of the ancient wooden structure that had long been due for renovation. Just as in 1861, the Catalan authorities, weighty bodies and faithful bourgeoisie rallied around and five years later a new Gran Teatre del Liceu was born, designed by the much acclaimed local architect Ignasi Solà Morales. Contrary to the wishes of many who saw it as an opportunity to build a showcase of new Catalan architecture, it is an extremely expensive reproduction of the old theatre with indulgent finishes, dripping in gilt, swathed in velvet and lined with marble. There are

no surprises, though some pleasing quirky features like the ceiling designed by contemporary artist Perejaume, and stage curtains by fashion designer Antonio Miró. It is also a long-overdue technological marvel with two stages able to cope with simultaneous performances.

As for its spirit, the new Liceu is more daring artistically, collaborating with avant-garde theatre companies like the Fura dels Baus or directors like Calitxo Beito. It has also initiated a policy of *òpera per tothom* in a bid to make opera available to a wider section of society, with more productions at affordable prices as well as foyer and children's performances.

Above: The façade of the opera house was not affected by the fire in 1994

From the moment it leaves Plaça Catalunya till it disgorges its flow of human traffic by the port, La Rambla is a constant parade of colourful characters. Apart from the transient street artists who are ruled by the weather, fashion or the state of their income, there is an assortment of perennial characters who are part of the very fabric of La Rambla. Famous for over 150 years as a place to promenade, it is now acquiring a new label as one of the longest theatres in the world.

Topping the bill and with regular appearances all the way down are the newspaper vendors in their distinctive green newsstands. Day and night whatever the weather they stand grimly

surveying the scene and always at the ready with the latest news. Also near the top is the intellectual shoe-shiner. Bronzed like a chestnut, when he is not squatting at someone's feet this wise Peruvian is reading the leaders in *El Pais* newspaper. Gathered around the entrance to the metro station at *aperitivo* time, or early evening, are crowds of retired men, twittering like sparrows, having a *tertulia*, an ingrained Spanish tradition of gathering together to discuss politics, football and putting the world to rights.

Human statues are the latest wave of performers in this elongated theatre. Some are highly professional, like the Jack-in-the-Box whose legs have disappeared but he still does not blink, or the metal cowboy standing on a wall by the Liceu metro. Others take the prize for humour, like the pink-haired lady in a leopard-skin coat who has been felled by a boulder on her way to the opera, or for sheer endurance – the increasingly pregnant 19th-century silver lady with her top-hatted partner.

The mobile performers are another inconsistent art form. Amongst the excellent is the South American with his concert-pianist frog. There are break-dancers, guitarists, a funky jazz musician with his piano on wheels – but the prize goes to the latest in fusion, a flamenco dancer who stamps on his *tablao* (portable dance floor) to the accompaniment of didgeridoos.

Beware the less desirable characters and rogues. The worst are the *trilleros* who invite you to guess which carrot-top the bean is under. With their stooges in the crowd they make it look simple, but no one ever beats them. At the first whistle from a lookout they disappear into thin air as the police cruise into sight only to find a bunch of gaping tourists. Pickpockets are another hazard, and find good fodder among the madding crowds distracted by one of the many acts.

In the last stretch are the literal artists, lined up to sketch your caricature or sell their works of art. And as a grand finale is Colon, the tallest statue of them all, never yet been known to blink.

Opposite: Street characters pulling in the crowds
Above and below: Human statues are the latest addition to the many characters found in La Rambla

Walk: Strolling down La Rambla

It would be foolish to try and go down Europe's most famous boulevard in any other way. Strolling is the way to do it, as the crush of people prevents brisk walking and you would be in danger of missing something in this ever-changing colourful spectacle. Go with the flow but take time to notice some of the sites outlined here.

Allow 1–2 hours so there is time to watch street performers, wander around La Boqueria market and maybe even pose as a model for an artist. All of the sights on this route are along La Rambla – begin at the Café Zurich on the corner of Plaça Catalunya or the metro exit at the top of La Rambla.

1 Font de Canaletes

This first stretch is named after its famous 19th-century cast-iron fountain loaded with symbolism for Barcelonans. A small plaque advises that anyone drinking from it will fall in love with the city and inevitably return. This popular fountain even has a low-lying spring for

Drink here and you will return to Barcelona

dogs. A favourite meeting place, its noisiest moments are when FC Barcelona has won the cup or the league and its over-excited fans assemble here to celebrate, chanting and blowing horns. *Walk south to just past C. Bonsucces.*

2 Reial Acadèmia de Ciències i Arts

Designed by Josep Domènech i Estapà at the end of the 19th century, this is still the headquarters of the Royal Academy of Science and Arts, and responsible for the Fabra Observatory on Tibidabo. For many years the clock was Barcelona's official timekeeper. Also housed here is the Teatre Poliorama which has a good weekend programme of children's theatre. *Continue south and cross over at C. de la Portaferrissa.*

3 Palau Moja

This elegant 18th-century neoclassical palace, taken over by the Department of

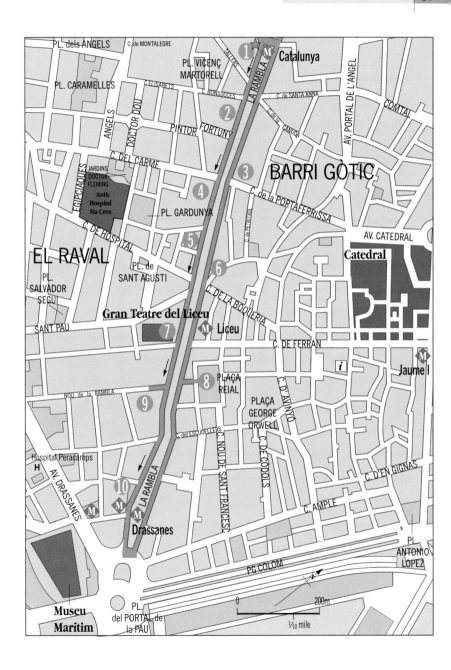

Boxes of fresh seafood for sale

Culture of the Generalitat, unfortunately can only be visited when it is hosting an exhibition. Much of its decorative detailing, both exterior and interior, can be glimpsed from La Rambla. Recently a major international sportswear brand has taken over the adjoining building, once the palace's garden, which along with the ubiquitous McDonald's on the corner of Ferran spell globalisation and threaten the beginning of the end of La Rambla. *Cross back over La Rambla.*

4 Palau de la Virreina

Built in 1778 for the Viceroy of Peru to be ready for his return from Lima. He died soon after, which is why it became known as the Palace of the Vicereine, his widow. Today it provides office space for the Institut de Cultura, the municipal cultural body. Its exhibition spaces on the ground floor and first floor have an active programme, and there is an extremely useful information service open to the public with leaflets on nearly everything going on culturally in the city, and a ticket office. It has a stylish souvenir shop, *La Botiga*, where

potential presents are strictly tasteful. *La Rambla 99. Tel: 933 161 000. www.bcn.es/cultura Continue south along La Rambla.*

5 La Boqueria

Also known as Mercat de Sant Josep, this is an essential stop on any itinerary. Dating from 1840, it is regarded as the most popular and colourful of Barcelona's many markets (*see pp150–51*) and along with Mercat Santa Caterina claims to be the oldest. Around 300 stalls spill over with fresh food, local vegetables, freshly picked ripe fruit and recently caught seafood. The intoxicating atmosphere of colours, aromas and ceaseless chatter is far more likely to make people return to Barcelona than the legendary water of Canaletes. Recent restoration work has highlighted its fine iron structure, *modernista* details and stained glass. *Open: Mon–Sat early in the morning–8pm. Cross the road.*

6 Casa Bruno Quadras

There are few examples of *modernista* architecture in the Old Town, but this is one of the most attractive. Designed by Josep Vilaseca in 1891, the decorative exterior shows clear signs of the oriental influence which left its mark on many *modernista* architects. Do not miss the umbrella. *Further along La Rambla, cross over opposite C. de Ferran.*

7 Gran Teatre del Liceu

The opera house with its dramatic history of fire and bombing is in full splendour since reopening in 1999

(*see pp82–3*). The old façade remains but its new casing now stretches down a whole block on La Rambla and back into the streets Sant Pau and Unió. The opera season has been extended including more dance and children's programmes. *La Rambla 51–59. Ticket booking: 902 533 353 or from abroad +34 932 746 411. www.liceubarcelona.com. Tours daily 10am–1pm.*
Further south, turn left into Plaça Reial.

8 Plaça Reial

A small opening on the left leads into the magnificent yet notorious Plaça Reial, built between 1848 and 1859, and supposedly inspired by Napoleonic French urban architecture. The elegance of its rigid geometric design and noble palm trees form a curious counterpoint to its decadent atmosphere and shady deals. Beware of pickpockets but be sure to visit it for a drink or a meal in one of the terrace cafés. It comes to life at night when retro bars like Glaciar regain their former *simpatico* atmosphere, and music bar Sidecar or jazz club Jamboree offer a good programme of live gigs. Los Tarantos is one of the most authentic flamenco clubs in town. In the side streets off the square are various laid-back lounge clubs. All life is here.
Go back to La Rambla, then turn right on Nou de la Rambla.

9 Palau Güell

Gaudí's loyal patron Eusebi Güell commissioned a town house from the architect in 1885 on a site just off La Rambla in Nou de la Rambla. Its façade may be overbearing to some, but once inside the beauty of its details is breathtaking. The world of fantasy on its roof should not be missed. *Nou de la Rambla. Closed for refurbishment until 2007.*
Returning to La Rambla, turn right.

10 Centre d'Art Santa Mònica

The final stretch of La Rambla is named after the convent which stood on the right, today strikingly converted into an exhibition centre with an attractive terrace café on the first floor. At street level is the cultural information centre of the Catalan government, with news about what is on in the arts in the whole of Catalonia. The narrow street Santa Mònica, once the stamping ground of the Barri Xino's famous prostitutes, manages to retain a bohemian atmosphere thanks to the evocative Bar Pastís, which has been playing the likes of Piaf and Jacques Brel since the 1950s. *Rambla Santa Monica 7. Tel: 933 162 810. www.cultura.gencat.es*

The Palau de la Virreina houses the municipal cultural information centre

Montjuïc

One of the distinguishing features of Barcelona, marking the gateway to the south, this bulky hill only 213m (700ft) high makes its presence felt almost everywhere in the city. Regenerated twice in the last 100 years as a venue for major international events, it nevertheless is still underused by local people. Its latest lease of life is coming from a new scheme, backed by the City Council, to open up neglected parts of the hill and make it more accessible so as to encourage more use of this large green space.

Statue of Sardana dancers

History

A pre-Roman civilisation lived here, and the Romans themselves built a temple to Jupiter on the hill, which could explain its name, a derivation of Mons Iovis. An alternative theory relates the name to the fact there was a Jewish cemetery here. The first serious landscaping of the hill was in preparation for the 1929 Universal Exposition, when many of today's monumental buildings were constructed. Some, like the Palau de Victòria Eugenia and the Palau d'Alfons XIII, are used by the Barcelona Trade Fair, while the Palau Nacional dominating the hilltop has been the home of the national art museum since 1934, now known as the MNAC (*see pp100–01*). The stadium over the hill behind the Palau Nacional was also built for the event, then refurbished and enlarged to cope with the next major event to take place on the hill, the XXV Olympiad in 1992.

Space age Palau Sant Jordi

Revival

The Barcelona Olympics may have been talked about ad nauseam but there is no denying the enormity of their impact, both in terms of international projection and their effect domestically. Not least to Montjuïc which was the main focus of events, from the spectacular opening ceremony in the stadium to its jubilant closure. It had to cope with hordes of people and millions of television viewers, so it had to work well and look good. A series of escalators was constructed to help move people around and the area around the stadium was landscaped, modern sculptures introduced, the space-age Palau Sant Jordi built by Isozaki, the sports university by Bofill and the striking Calatrava communications tower, as well as swimming pools and athletics tracks. It all looked very sleek, and still does. Sports enthusiasts can visit the stadium and see the exhibition on the event in the Galeria Olímpica behind.

Galeria Olímpica.
Open: Tue–Sat 10am–1pm, 4–6pm,
Sun 10am–2pm.

Cultural centre
The hill has been associated with cultural events for many years. Apart from the prized art collection in the Palau Nacional, there is the world-class Fundació Joan Miró and the new Caixa Forum, while architects from around the world flock to the Mies van der Rohe pavilion (*for all these see pp98–101*). In addition there are some good museums.
Museu d'Arqueologia de Catalunya,
Passeig Santa Madrona 39–41.
Open: Tue–Sat 9.30am–7pm,
Sun 10am–2.30pm.
Museu Etnològic, Passeig Santa Madrona.
Open: Tue–Sun 10am–2pm. Admission
charge for both.

A visit to the Fundació Joan Miró is a must

Montjuïc also has a strong theatrical tradition. Plays and concerts held in the 'Greek' amphitheatre, also built for 1929, are a highlight of the annual Grec Festival, a summer festival of theatre, dance and music that runs from late June until early August. It is a magical setting on a hot summer night. Just at the foot of the hill on Lleida is 'Theatre Town', a complex of theatres which aims to provide a range of performances, from studio workshops to large-scale productions. The Teatre Lliure is now based here.

Castell de Montjuïc

At the summit is the Montjuïc castle which can be reached by cable car (temporarily closed for refurbishment) from Avinguda Miramar. This sturdy castle dates from the 17th century, though after being attacked by Bourbon troops it had to be rebuilt in the late 18th century. A tragic part of Catalonia's history took place here in 1940, when General Lluís Companys, president of the Generalitat, was executed by Franco's troops. It marked the beginning of the dark period of nearly 40 years of dictatorship. The castle houses a military museum with antique weapons, notably an 18th-century collection from Ripoll, uniforms and miniature soldiers. *Open: Tue–Sun 9.30am–5.30pm, Mar–Oct until 8pm. Admission charge.*

Cable car to the Montjuïc castle

Fountains of the Palau Nacional

New plans

The latest phase in the development of this city hill is the Council's plan to encourage its use, claiming that few capitals can boast such an asset. New bus routes will make it easier to reach the hill, and once there new parts are being opened for walking or exploration, like the Camí del Mar. This is an attractive footpath that runs from just beneath the castle along the sea side of the hill, giving panoramic views of the busy working port. The old funfair has been landscaped and opened as the Joan Brossa Gardens, in memory of the charismatic poet/artist whose poetic sculptures can be seen all over the city. It has been planted with wild flowers and has imaginative creative games for children. The Botanical Gardens opened a few years ago are now getting established and worth visiting and new footpaths are being developed. The aim is to offer a day out in the fresh air combining culture, sport and nature.

THE M CARD

The M Card is part of the new scheme to promote Montjuïc. It is a day pass which for about €20 opens up the hillside to you, from the Miró Foundation to the Picornell Olympic swimming pool. It allows you free admission to all the museums, events in the Caixa Forum, and the Poble Espanyol (the Spanish Village). You can travel around by cable car or tourist train, and at weekends you can use bicycles provided, all for free. After an exhausting day on the hill you can then use the pass for the theatre, either the Teatre Lliure or Mercat de Flors, if tickets are not sold out.

The M Card can be bought at any of the collaborating entities, the Tourist Office or through www.servicaixa.com. Information point: Pg. Santa Madiona 28.
Tel: 932 892 830.

When enjoying the tangy air, delicious seafood and sunshine of Barcelona's waterfront, even long-time residents find it hard to remember that little more than a decade ago all this was a wasteland of derelict factories, warehouses and railway tracks. Barcelona is what it is today thanks to the Olympic Games of 1992. The Games brought far more than the promotion of Barcelona as a cosmopolitan capital, and far more than the stylish new residential neighbourhood of the Olympic Village and flagship sports facilities.

What the 1992 Olympics made possible was quite simply the revival of the entire city. Barcelona's determined bid to host them was a key element in the far-reaching municipal policy implemented after the first democratic elections of 1979. Staging the games was the key piece in a master plan to channel hard-earned money back into Barcelona for the benefit of its citizens.

During General Franco's dictatorship, with its *laissez-faire* economic policy and fierce repression of the Catalan identity, hard-working industrialised Barcelona and its metropolitan belt continued to be the economic powerhouse of Spain, and immigrants from the impoverished south poured in. Chronically underfunded, Barcelona became one of the world's most densely populated cities. Cheap housing was thrown up without a thought to infrastructure or amenities. Barcelona was choking to death.

Nothing less than total regeneration was the aim of the socialists who won the City Council in 1979. They initiated

a new forward-looking urban policy, putting people and quality of life before profit. Subsidies were offered for restoring façades, green spaces were recovered, public amenities built. The hosting of the Olympic Games provided the ideal framework, the perfect way to obtain financing for the ambitious project that encompassed the whole city and its environs.

Radical improvement of the road system included the desperately needed ring road (Les Rondes) and expressway (Túnels de Vallvidrera) to the towns on the other side of Collserola. The airport was enlarged and innumerable buildings renovated. The waterfront and beaches were rescued and redeveloped. New buildings included the twin skyscrapers forming the gateway to the Olympic Port, Norman Foster's communications tower on Collserola and Calatrava's on Montjuïc, Isozaki's Palau Sant Jordi... the list goes on. During the dusty years of demolition and construction, the Council repeatedly promised disrupted citizens that it was the Barcelona of the future that was being built. Since the Games, the socialists have continued to hold the Council and to execute the development policy. That Barcelona is now a number-one destination has clearly proved them right.

Opposite: The Olympic Stadium
Above: A detail of the Palau Sant Jordi
Below: Diving events were impressive with a backdrop of the city

The Spanish Village on Montjuïc is one of the city's most popular sites, attracting 1.5 million visitors a year, most of them Spanish. This kitsch collection of fake buildings from different parts of the country has worn the passage of time with some dignity. Renovations in the late 1980s created within its walls one of the trendiest bars in the city and as it passes its 75th anniversary its owners see it becoming a centre of cultural and artisanal excellence.

The village was among many great fakes created for the 1929 World Exhibition on Montjuïc that included Venetian towers, Renaissance palaces and a Greek Theatre. It has around 120 houses, each from a different part of Spain. The architects, Francesc Folguera and Ramon Reventós, aided by the critic Miguel Utrillo and the artist Javier Nogués, had travelled the country to research their project, looking at typical houses built between the 11th and 20th centuries. The result is a surprisingly harmonious community centred on an arcaded Plaça Major, with pavement cafés and a town hall from Valderrobles in Teruel. There are balconies from the Basque country, stone houses from Extramadura, courtyards from Seville and a selection of buildings from the pilgrims' route to Santiago de Compostella. Today, people who are restoring old houses even come to carry out their research.

The crafts of the nation were also shown in the original exhibition, and later there were two museums showing popular traditions, crafts and the graphic

arts. The artisan workshops have been revived and there are nearly 40 of them engaged in printing, glass blowing and other traditional activities. The village, which is privately owned, has ambitions to become an 'artisanal reference centre'. There are also three art schools and several businesses based in the buildings.

Souvenir shops, a bank and tourist information office add to the theme-park feel, but Barcelonans make it their entertainment place of choice in the evenings and at weekends when flamenco, audiovisual programmes and other shows are regularly staged. There are also some 17 restaurants to choose from and a number of bars.

The whole complex is wrapped around by a copy of the 11th-century walls of Àvila, in central Spain, with its Puerto de San Vicente forming the entrance. Inside one of the gate's towers is the Torres de Àvila, a bar created in 1990 by the architect Alfredo Arribas and the designer Javier Mariscal, which for a while was the trendiest place in town. With myriad rooms and a roof terrace giving spectacular views over the city, it is worth checking out. Today the venue is a dance club.

Just outside the walls are a new sculpture garden and a replica monastery from the province of Girona. *Marqués de Comillas, Parc de Montjuïc. Tel: 933 257 866. www.poble-espanyol.com. Open: Mon 9am–8pm,*

Tue–Thur 9am–2am, Fri–Sat 9am–4am, Sun 9am–midnight. Admission charge. Metro: Espanya. Bus: 13 or 50.

Above: Artworks are on sale in the village centred on Plaça Major (opposite)
Below: Santiago Cathedral in miniature

Walk: Montjuïc

The best way to visit the key sites on Montjuïc hill is on foot, using the escalators for the steep bits. Currently undergoing a revival, more gardens and green spaces are becoming accessible to the public, and a new walkway has opened near the castle, overlooking the port and the Mediterranean beyond. For the adventurous and energetic there are infinite walks on this hill, one of Barcelona's landmarks.

Allow half a day.

Start in Plaça Espanya, easily reached by metro lines 1 or 3.

1 Plaça Espanya

This busy roundabout is a gateway out of Barcelona, funnelling traffic south while the incoming traffic roars underneath it, and a strategic point for visitors to Montjuïc and the two million visitors a year that flood into the Fira de Barcelona, the Trade Fair site along Avinguda Reina Maria Cristina. Its central statue was erected for the 1929 Universal Exposition. Entitled 'Spain', it was designed by Jujol, one of Gaudí's collaborators, though his usual original *modernista* style was evidently repressed, probably by demands from central government in Madrid who were very influential in the Exposition. The former bullring Las Arenas, dating from 1900, is going the way of many old characters in this rapidly developing city, and is about to be reborn as a Richard Rodgers commercial centre. The twin 'Venetian' towers were the main entrance to the 1929 Exposition.

Go south on Av Reina Maria Cristina to Pl Carlos Buïgas.

2 Font Màgica

On the first esplanade is the much-loved Magic Fountain. This was designed by Carlos Buïgas in 1929, but is still plying away with its colourful musical show from Thursday to Sunday evenings between June and September (8pm–midnight), Friday and Saturday in winter, 7–9pm.

Turn left on Av Marquès de Comillas.

3 Caixa Forum

At this stage take an optional but recommended detour a short way along the Avinguda Marquès de Comillas to the magnificent Caixa Forum, the new cultural centre of the affluent 'La Caixa' Foundation. Also known as the Casaramona, it was an award-winning textile factory designed in 1911 by Puig i Cadafalch. It has a stunning new glass entrance, designed by Isozaki, leading into a huge space on several levels offering concerts, exhibitions and lectures, along with a media library open to the public, and the Foundation's vast contemporary art collection. The building alone is worth visiting, a fine

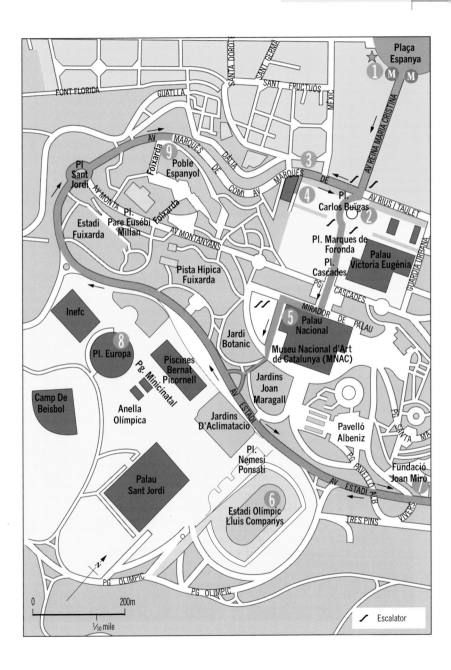

example of Catalan *modernista* industrial architecture.

Av Marquès de Comillas 6–8. Tel: 902 223 040. www.fundacio.lacaixa.es. Open: Tue–Sun 10am–8pm. Free admission. Check local listings for arts and music festivals held here.
Cross Av Marquès de Comillas.

4 Pavelló Mies van der Rohe

Another extraordinary architectural gem, once described as a building 'which will one day be remembered as the most beautiful of those built throughout the 20th century'. Designed by Mies van der Rohe as the German pavilion for the 1929 Exposition, it seems totally modern in stark contrast with the other elaborate buildings built on the hill at the same time. Dismantled after the Exposition, it was rebuilt in the 1980s by a group of Barcelona architects, utterly faithful to the original.
Open: daily 10am–8pm. Admission charge. Return to Magic Fountain and ride the escalators up the hill past more 1929 pavilions now used for trade fairs. Retrace your steps and turn right into Pl Carlos Buïgas. Continue south towards the Palau Nacional, turning right on Mirador de Palau, then left.

5 Palau Nacional

This monumental building that dominates Montjuïc has been the home of the Museu Nacional d'Art de Catalunya

The new Caixa Forum offering entertainment for all

(the MNAC) since 1934. Its highly prized collection of Catalan Romanesque art, much of it carefully rescued from village churches in the Pyrenees, is breathtakingly beautiful. It has recently been magnificently restored to house 1,000 years of Catalan art up to the 20th century including photography, stamps and coins and part of the Thyssen-Bornemisza collection (*see p136*).

Go south past the Jardins Joan Maragall until you reach Av Estadi. Turn left here, and the stadium is further along on the right.

6 Olympic stadium and complex

More escalators behind the Palau Nacional lead up to Avinguda de l'Estadi. Here the mountain opens up to the southeast and the Olympic complex spreads over it. The high-tech Palau Sant Jordi, another Isozaki piece, was used for the indoor events and now divides its time between mega rock concerts and sundry sports championships. The Olympic stadium was adapted from the original 1929 stadium to accommodate 55,000 spectators.

Tel: 934 262 089. Open: daily 10am–8pm, in winter until 6pm. Free admission. Continue in the same direction along Av Estadi.

7 Fundació Joan Miró

A short walk along the road is one of the largest collections in the world of Miró's art, housed in a spectacular museum designed by his close friend Josep Lluís Sert. The Mediterranean light that floods into the building shows Miró's work at its best. The restaurant

has an attractive courtyard which is very pleasant for lunch.

Av Miramar 1. Tel: 934 439 470. www.bcn.fjmiro.es. Open: Tue–Sat 10am–7pm, Thur 10am–9.30pm, Sun 10am–2.30pm. Admission charge. Retrace your steps along Av Estadi, continuing past the Jardi Botanic. Pl Europa is on the left.

8 Torre Calatrava

Another landmark, this communication tower was designed by Valencian architect Santiago Calatrava for the 1992 Olympics. It is one of the symbols of the new Barcelona that has been projected to the world during and since the Games.

Carry on along Av Estadi, past Pl Sant Jordi, back to Av Marquès de Comillas.

9 Poble Espanyol

Another legacy of the 1929 Exposition, the Spanish Village was built to show the different regional architectures of Spain along with various arts and crafts (*see pp96–7*). Something of a pastiche, it still draws the crowds and is a big hit with children. In its latest lease of life it has become a popular nightlife venue, especially for late-night dancing in summer. Some of the concerts during the Grec Summer Festival are held in its Plaza Mayor.

From the Poble Espanyol you can head back past the Olympic stadium and the Fundació Joan Miró, from where you can catch the funicular to metro line 3, just along Avinguda Miramar. Or you can continue along the Avinguda Marquès de Comillas back to the Magic Fountain.

Parc de la Ciutadella

The city's largest park blossomed from one of the most
hated symbols of the power of Madrid – a fortress built by
the conquering Bourbons. For two centuries it was a
gloomy, forbidding place and when it finally came down
nobody mourned its passing. From then on everyone
could enjoy a new pleasure garden – and a World Fair that
celebrated a new era.

Fontseré's formal gardens

After the besieged city of Barcelona was
finally defeated by Felipe V's Franco-
Spanish troops in 1714, a fortress was
built as barracks for 8,000 troops to
make sure that disagreements with the
capital never led to warfare again. It was
just one of many draconian measures
introduced by the new Bourbon ruler,
including the banning of the Catalan
language and the closing of the city's
university.

Oppressive prison
Forty streets and more than 1,200
houses were demolished to make way
for the star-shaped fortress designed by
Prosper Verboom, and the inhabitants
were only belatedly given new housing
in Barceloneta (*see pp32–3*). In fact the
building was never used as a barracks,
but it became a prison, used by
Napoleon's troops when they invaded
and afterwards for liberals opposed

A playground in the park, which attracts families with its pleasant gardens and boating lake

Giraffes in the city zoo, which occupies the southern part of the park

to the government in Madrid. It was therefore with enormous zeal that the place was torn down in 1869 when the country's liberal leader General Prim, himself a Catalan, gave the lands to the city to turn into a public park. In gratitude the city erected an equestrian statue of him in its centre.

Exhibition space

The main architect for the park was Josep Fontseré i Mestres who, with a team of designers that included a fledgling Gaudí, set about producing lawns, lakes, plots, parterres and the Cascada, a fountain with Neptune, sea horses and a grotto. The grand plan all came together in time for the Universal Exhibiton of 1888, when early *modernista* buildings were added to the 19th-century grandeur. The exhibition was open for just six months, attracting around 6,000 people a day. They came

to ride in a hot-air balloon and gape at such novelties as a giant sculpture of Mozarella cheese as well as to visit palaces devoted to science, agriculture and the arts. When the exhibition closed most of the buildings were pulled down.

Verboom's arsenal, meanwhile, had not been destroyed but remodelled, and it is now occupied by the Catalan parliament, guarded by Mossos d'Esquadra, the Catalan police. Outside this building in Plaça de Armes, laid out by the French landscape gardener Jean Forestier, is an elegant sculpture by Josep Llimona in the middle of a pond. But the park's best loved sculpture stands inside the zoo, which arrived at the turn of the last century. The fashionable *Dama del Paraigua* (*Woman with an Umbrella*), by Roig i Soler, holds out her hand as rain cascades down over her umbrella. She has become a charming mascot of the city.

Walk: Parc de la Ciutadella

There is something for everyone in this tranquil leisure ground that is enjoyed by Barcelonans all the year round. Parakeets escaped from the Rambla squawk in its trees and buggies are pushed around its paths among flowerbeds and plantations. The lake attracts idle rowers, there are benches for the weary and lawns for lovers to lie on. Add a zoo and a museum or two, and the picture of a leisurely outing is complete.

Allow 3 hours or more, depending on how much diverts your attention.

Start at the Arc de Triomf (Metro line 1). Leave by gate near Wellington for the Ciutadella–Villa Olímpica metro (line 4) or tram.

The Umbracle is full of tropical plants

1 Arc de Triomf

Based on Napoleon's triumphal arch in Paris, this one was erected as the entrance to the 1888 Universal Exhibition that filled the park. Still in an imposing position at the end of the long avenue of Passeig Sant Joan and near the law courts, the red-brick and white-marble building in a *mudéjar* style remains impressive. It was designed by Josep Vilaseca i Casanovas with a frieze by Josep Reynés depicting Barcelona welcoming visitors to the city. Stroll down the elegant Passeig Lluis Companys to the main park entrance. *Walk southeast on PG Lluis Companys, crossing PG Pujades.*

2 Museu de Zoòlogia

The zoological museum is housed in the Castell dels Tres Dragons (Castle of the

Three Dragons), which was designed by Domènech i Montaner as the café-restaurant for the Universal Exhibition. Contemporary exhibitions are held here to counter the musty feel of an old-fashioned collection of molluscs, insects and invertebrates. The nearby **Museu de Geologia**, with a collection of minerals, fossils and rocks and an explanation of the region's substrata, was the city's first museum, built in 1878, and it has an equally 19th-century feel. They now both come under the name Museu de les Ciències Naturals de la Ciutadella.
Passeig de Picasso. Tel: 933 196 912. www.bcn.es/museusciencies. Open: Tue–Sun 10am–2pm. Admission charge; combined tickets for both museums available.

3 Hivernacle

Between the two museums is a delightful hothouse filled with tropical plants. There is a bar and a good restaurant inside. It stays open late and has jazz and concert evenings in the summer months, which are well worth looking out for. It is complemented on the other side of the Museu de Geologia by the **Umbracle**, another hothouse of wood, brick and elegant iron pillars designed by Fontseré, the park's principal architect.
Passeig de Picasso. Tel: 934 243 809. Heading further into the Parc de la Ciutadella, go around the Pl Les Armes to the Parlament de Catalunya.

A mammoth outing for a child in the zoo

4 Parlament de Catalunya

Once the arsenal of the 18th-century citadel, this building now houses the Catalan parliament, a poetic symbol of the return to a degree of independence for Catalonia from central government. Until recently it shared the space with the Modern Art Museum whose collection is now in the MNAC (*see pp100–01*). *Continue through the park to the zoo.*

Parc de la Ciutadella fountain, an ideal place to relax

5 Parc Zoològic

The city zoo is a favourite attraction and its star performer for many years was the much loved Snowflake, an Albino gorilla with attitude whose descendants are now being raised here. Make sure a visit coincides with the dolphin show. The zoo has an enlightened programme of conservation and collaborates on a number of international and European programmes for breeding and preserving species threatened with extinction. There is a plan to move the zoo further up the coast to the Riva Besós, and turn the site into a further recreation area of the park. *Parc de la Ciutadella. Tel: 932 256 780. www.zoobarcelona.com. Open: 10am–5pm; May–Aug 9.30am–7.30pm. Admission charge.*

Snowflake, the most famous past resident of the zoo

The attractive Hivernacle is a pleasant spot for a drink

Park Güell

The Park Güell is a supreme example of Gaudí's bold genius, built at a time when the use of local rustic stone and indigenous plants and the recycling of stone and ceramics were seen as utterly eccentric. Originally intended to be a garden city, probably inspired by models of the time that emerged as a reaction to the filthy, ugly cities of the industrial revolution, it integrates architecture and nature in a whole of unique loveliness.

Columns at Park Güell

In the late 19th century the cultured aristocrat Eusebi Güell bought a property on a bare hillside above Gràcia and commissioned Gaudí, with whom he shared both aesthetic and nationalist ideas, to carry out the project. The area intended for communal amenities was practically the only part built, since the project foundered through lack of interest from the conventional Eixample-dwelling bourgeoisie, with only a couple of plots sold. After Güell's death in 1918, his heirs sold the property to the City Council for it to be turned into a public park. It was declared a UNESCO World Heritage Site in 1984 and has since been restored.

The 'fairy-tale' architecture and flowing forms that are almost synonymous with Gaudí are underpinned by meticulous calculation of every single technical detail. The estate

This colourful, ceramic lizard is one of Gaudí's most famous visual symbols

Trencadís work on the undulating bench

was divided into triangular lots linked by paths and viaducts winding round the hill. The three viaducts formed a brick service structure which Gaudí then clad in local stone and endowed with sculptural value. The result is a merging of nature and stone, with tunnels, bridges and lookouts to surprise the visitor. While the lower viaduct is sober, the upper ones grow increasingly ornamented, with double colonnades, a wave-like inner profile, and a texture resembling molten wax. The top viaduct is twisting and heavy, with chubby columns and sculpted jardinières. The ensemble was planned to accommodate climbing and hanging plants.

While the architectural elements of the park clearly get the most attention, it also reveals Gaudí as an ecologist before his time. The original vegetation was very sparse, and he planned a Mediterranean wood, with native species that would proliferate spontaneously. Thick pine groves and existing trees were reinforced by various plantations and ornamental species with spectacular blossoms. The rest is now a dense wood, carpeted with shrubs and crossed by dirt paths and stone stairways. The park contains several listed trees, including an ancient carob growing in the middle of the path on the central viaduct. Gaudí bumped into the tree as the work progressed and refused to have it cut down. The wood is also home to more than 60 species of bird, some permanent residents, others migratory.

At one end of the park (going left from the entrance), where the church was to be built, Gaudí made a stone promontory with a rather primitive aspect, with three crosses at its summit, reached by a rough flight of steps. At the back of the park on the other side of the hill is the traditional fountain of Sant Salvador, remodelled in 1984. The spacious plaza has a children's playground and a fabulous view over the city.

One of the gatehouses to the park

Antoní Gaudí i Cornet

With fluid lines, decorative ironwork and soaring flights of fancy, the architecture of Antoní Gaudí i Cornet is a symbol of Barcelona. Devoted both to the church and to Catalan nationalism, he was a master mason, painter and sculptor who relied on his own hands and eyes rather than on measurements and calculations. His organic buildings are a heady mix of styles, a peculiar Catalan neo-Gothic.

Gaudí was born in 1852, and while attending Barcelona's School of Architecture he worked in creating the new Parc de la Ciutadella. After graduating, his first and only municipal commission was for street lamps in the Plaça Reial, which are still in place.

After two important building projects, Casa Vicens in Barcelona and El Capricho

in northern Spain, Gaudí had his first commission from his most generous patron, the industrialist Count Eusebi Güell. The commission was for what is now known as the Güell Pavilion, on the count's farm estate in Pedralbes. A typical Catalan polymath, Güell was also a politician and supporter of the arts. His home in Carrer Nou de la Rambla was always full of social gatherings and in the 1880s Gaudí designed a new extension. The resulting Palau Güell (*see p89*), Gaudí's only building in the old town, was a gloomy Gothic masterpiece and Güell declared that he liked it less and less the higher it grew. Famously, he never ventured on to its elaborate roof to see its glazed and decorated chimneys.

But he liked it enough to give Gaudí another major commission, Park Güell (*see pp108–9*). It was to be a model community with 60 houses but only two were completed, one of which Gaudí made his home – it is now the Casa-Museu Gaudí. And when Güell installed a new textile plant at Santa Coloma de Cervello, 17km (11 miles) west of Barcelona, he asked Gaudí to build a church, but the death of the wealthy patron in 1918 left it incomplete.

Bellesguard, a severe Gothic mansion beneath Tibidabo (*Carrer de Bellesguard 16–20*), was completed in 1902, and his most restrained building, the Casa Calvet (*Carrer de Casp 48*), was finished two years later. This was followed by Casa Batlló in Passeig de Gràcia and his final commission, Casa Milà, known as La Pedrera (*see p68*). These two Eixample showcases both have extraordinary Gaudí interiors.

After completing La Pedrera in 1910, unwashed and unpaid, Gaudí devoted

himself entirely to the Sagrada Família (*see pp114–15*), a project he had already been involved with for 17 years. He ended his days here as a recluse, living in a hut on the site, and when he was run down by a tram in Gran Via in 1926 and taken to hospital, he remained unrecognised for two days, dying shortly afterwards. The building had been the climax of his life's labour and with it he ensured that his name would forever be linked with the city.

Left top: La Pedrera, Gaudí's apartment block on Passeig de Gràcia
Left and opposite: towers and colonnades in Park Güell
Above: Casa Batlló in Passeig de Gràcia

Walk: Park Güell

In Gaudí's Park Güell, all the architectural elements blend effortlessly with nature. Barcelona's famous visual symbols such as the 'gingerbread house', the mosaic lizard and the monumental plaza combine with fabulous views over the city and quieter stretches of Mediterranean wood to make this a unique, unmissable wonder.

Allow 3 hours.

The walk begins at the main entrance to the park on Carrer Olot, reached by bus 24 or metro (line 3) to Lesseps.

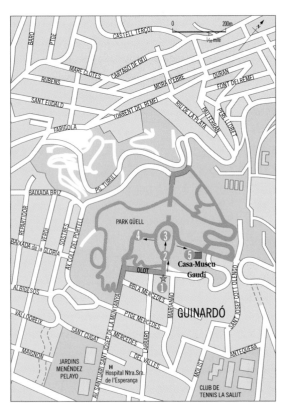

1 Entrance

The gate, by Gaudí, originally belonged to the Casa Vicens and was put here in 1965. With their curved lines and mosaic ceramic roofs, the two pavilions flanking the entrance immediately take us into a fairy-tale world. In fact everything in the park is filled with symbolic elements. One of these buildings was designed as living quarters for the janitors of the garden city and the other for visitor reception and telephones.
Walk straight ahead.

2 Staircase

The monumental staircase was conceived as the formal entrance to the communal areas of the garden city, but its scale is softened by the ornamentation, including the famous water-spitting lizard or dragon, and the vegetation.

It is difficult to know what mythical world Gaudí had in his head, but he still thought of every practical detail: the vault to the right of the staircase was to provide shelter on rainy days.

3 Sala Hipòstila and Plaça de la Natura

The Hypostyle Hall was originally intended as the marketplace and the spectacular plaza above it as the main communal space for cultural activities. The hall has 86 columns 6.16m (20ft) tall; the outer ones are inclined and act as buttresses. Gaudí's touch is visible in their irregular arrangement. Some of the columns enclose gutters which drain rainwater from the plaza into an underground tank, the lizard being the overflow pipe. The columns partly hold up the plaza, a real amphitheatre overlooking the city, edged by the famous undulating bench decorated with *trencadís* (pieces of ceramic).
Leave the left-hand side of the Hypostyle Hall.

4 Viaducte de la Bugadera

The natural, organic forms of the viaducts conceal meticulous calculations of differing inclines for pedestrians and carriages. The 3km (2 miles) of paths follow a formal logic which Gaudí breaks now and then with playful details, such as the lone figure of a washerwoman. The original figure held a washboard and was later reconstructed.

Follow the long route around the park via the Turó de les Menes with its three crosses.
Return to the Hypostyle Hall and exit the right-hand side.

The famous serpentine bench was mostly the work of Jujol

5 Casa-Museu Gaudí

This building, by Francesc Berenguer, was the showhouse. Gaudí bought it with his meagre savings and lived in it with his father and niece until he went to live on-site at the Sagrada Família. In his will he stipulated that the house be sold and the proceeds go to the building of that church. It was bought by the Friends of Gaudí in 1963 to be turned into a museum. In it one can see furniture and rooms of the period, reproductions of Gaudí pieces and a small garden with a pergola.
Park and museum open daily:
10am–8pm (summer),
10am–6pm (winter).
Admission charge to house only.

Sagrada Família

One of the world's most extraordinary churches, the Sagrada Família has been more or less a building site for more than a century. Gaudí's lofty plans have been scaled back considerably in an effort to see it completed. But it still has a long way to go.

Detail, Sagrada Família

The idea for a new church in Barcelona came from a local bookseller, Josep Bocabella, who had founded a religious society devoted to St Joseph and a better understanding between workers and employers. The site was purchased and the architect hired, but Francesc de Paula Villar i Lozano, who produced a design based on a Gothic cathedral, had completed only a small section of the crypt when he fell out with Bocabella in 1883, a year after work began. Antoní Gaudí, then 31, was asked to take over.

Grand plans

Gaudí's plans for the Temple Expiatori de la Sagrada Família (The Holy Family Church of the Atonement) grew by the day. He conceived a huge building 60m (197ft) wide at the transept with a nave 90m (295ft) long and an external ambulatory or cloister that would entirely surround the building. The nave would look like a forest of stone pillars and the stone seats designed to seat 1,300 were to be placed close together to prevent people crossing their legs. By the time of his death in 1926 only the crypt, the apse, one tower and the beautifully sculpted Nativity façade – the one in all the postcards – had been completed. The centre of the building had become a stonemasons' quarry, and though he left no detailed plans he made it clear that those who came after him should have the freedom to do what they thought best for the building.

Work on the church stopped during the Civil War, when models were broken

The towers with mosaics and tinkling bells

and drawings destroyed. It resumed in 1952, getting a boost in the 1980s when the Passion façade was created with sculptures by Josep Maria Subirachs, an avowed atheist. They seem at odds with Gaudí's Nativity figures, which are being continued by a Japanese sculptor, Etsuro Sotoo. Bright Venetian mosaics have been added to the top of the playful tinkling bell towers, and to avoid the 400 steps in the spiral staircases a lift rises to the giddy heights of the towers where there are bird's-eye views of the church and the city. In the crypt, where Gaudí is buried, there is a museum and an altar for services.

Future work

The south façade, designed to be the main entrance to the building, and the entire nave are yet to be built. It is still envisaged that a central spire, much taller than the city cathedral's, will be surrounded by four large towers representing the Evangelists. The weight of all this additional stonework will require a foundation of thousands of tons of concrete.

The debate about whether it is actually worth finishing the workers' church or if it is better just to leave it as a monument to its creator has gone on since Gaudí's death. In the meantime the building creeps ever heavenward. *Mallorca 401. Tel: 932 073 031. www.sagradafamilia.org. Open: Oct–Mar 9am–6pm, Apr–Sept 9am–8pm. Admission charge. Metro: Sagrada Família (lines 2 and 5). Bus: 15, 19, 33, 43, 44, 50, 51.*

Entrance to the Sagrada Família – Gaudí never thought in straight lines

Walk: around Sagrada Família

Too many visitors flock to the Sagrada Família by metro, bus or taxi, take the obligatory tour and return exhausted to their hotels, missing some of the other *modernista* sites in the vicinity. This walk covers a few of these designed by contemporaries of Gaudí.

Allow 3 hours.

Take metro (line 5) to Hospital de Sant Pau or line 4 to Guinardó. The walk begins at the entrance to the hospital on Sant Antoni Maria Claret.

1 Hospital de la Santa Creu i Sant Pau

When this quite magnificent complex was built in 1901 it was the most advanced hospital in Europe. Designed by Lluís Domènech i Montaner, it has separate pavilions set amongst gardens, connected by a subterranean labyrinth. Visitors can wander around and enjoy the tile-work and elaborate details which are the hallmark of this architect.
Head south down Av Gaudí.

2 Sagrada Família

Take the opportunity to appreciate the exterior of Barcelona's most famous building from all angles, but save the details and tower climbing for a separate visit (*see pp114–15*). Walk past the Gloria façade on Mallorca and glimpse the Passion façade sculpted by contemporary artist Subirachs. The park opposite often has outdoor markets.
Exit via Pl Sagrada Família, turning right on Mallorca then left on Sicilia. Turn right on Diagonal and walk to the junction with PG Sant Joan.

3 Casa Macaya

Designed in 1901 by Josep Puig i Cadafalch. Originally a town house, it now houses the La Caixa Foundation offices. Be sure to see the magnificent courtyard.
Passeig Sant Joan 106.
Continue west on Diagonal.

4 Casa Terrades

This part of the Diagonal shows the Eixample at its most elegant, part of the so-called *Quadrat d'Or* or Golden Square where the most prized *modernista* buildings are found. Interesting hallways, jealously guarded by the *portero* or *portera* (caretaker), are a tempting appetiser to the world within. The Casa Terrades, also designed by Puig i Cadafalch in 1903, is no exception. Popularly known as the Casa de les Punxes (the house of spikes), it is supposedly the only detached building in the Eixample. It is not open to the public but there is plenty to see at street level in this fairy-tale building.

Av Diagonal 416–420.
Carry on along Diagonal, beyond Pau
Claris.

5 Casa Asia

This is one of the most elaborate and
decorative Puig i Cadafalch buildings.
The Palau Baró de Quadras (1906)
was for years the home of the Music
Museum. Just reopened as Asia House,
it holds exhibitions and other events
always with an oriental theme and
invites people to wander around its
beautifully restored interior. Do not
miss the rear of the building which backs
on to Rosselló.
Av Diagonal 373/Carrer Rosselló 279.
www.casaasia.es. Open: Mon–Sat
10am–8pm, Sun 10am–2pm. Free
admission.

6 Casa Comalat

Another building which has to be seen
from front and behind. Designed in 1911
by the lesser-known Salvador Valeri.
Av Diagonal 442.
Turn right on PG Gràcia.

7 Casa Fuster

An elegant, quite subdued building, one
of Domènech i Montaner's last pieces
(1911). It wraps around the corner
marking the end of Passeig de Gràcia,
with spectacular views down the whole
length of one of Barcelona's most elegant
streets. Recently opened as a luxury hotel,
its *modernista* details are highlighted.
Passeig de Gràcia 132. Continue up Gran
de Gràcia to explore the 'village' of Gràcia
(see pp72–5) or return to the junction
with Diagonal.

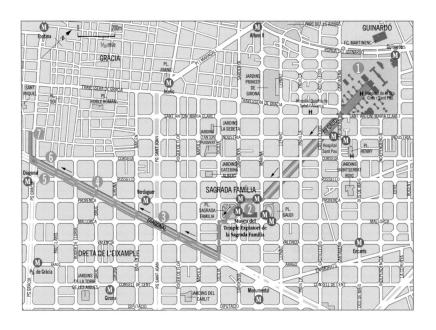

Sarrià and Pedralbes

Less than ten minutes by train from Plaça Catalunya, the former village of Sarrià is now part of the urban sprawl but still manages to retain a sense of village life with its pretty alleyways, small terraced houses with plants spilling over iron fences, and some ancient establishments. It provides an appealing contrast to the well-trodden tourist track and a good place for lunch or as a stepping-stone up to the Collserola park.

Relax in the village-like tranquillity of Sarrià

The main square, Plaça de Sarrià, is dominated by the church of Sant Vicenç. Nearby is the attractive covered market,

Sarrià's main square overlooked by Sant Vicenç church

dating from 1911, which perpetuates the sense of village life. Running down from the Plaça is the main street, Major de Sarrià, where a pause at Bar Tomàs (*Major de Sarrià 49*) is essential. People make the pilgrimage from all over the city for its famed *patatas bravas* (fried potatoes served with spicy sauce or mayonnaise). Alternatively plan a visit around lunchtime so you can eat *canalons* or one of the other home-made dishes in family-run Casa Joana (*No 59*). The side streets are worth exploring to find dimly lit shops from another era and turn-of-the-century villas.

Beyond the nucleus, however, it becomes obvious that this is uptown and upmarket, and a desirable residential area. The official district is Sarrià–Sant Gervasi which comprises the even more desirable Pedralbes at one extreme and towards Tibidabo the Sant Gervasi area, with the highest concentration of private schools, hospitals and four-wheel-drives in Barcelona. In amongst the smart apartment blocks with manicured

Funicular travel makes Barcelona's steep hills more accessible

gardens are some interesting examples of *modernista* architecture, including two Gaudí buildings: the extraordinary convent Escola de les Teresianes (*Ganduxer 85–105*) which can be visited on Saturdays, and a private house Torre Bellesguard (*Bellesguard 20*).

The grass is definitely greener in Pedralbes, the air is much fresher and the density of population dramatically lower than in the Eixample or Ciutat Vella. It is favoured by expats, diplomats and even royals. What it gains in air quality and reduced noise pollution, though, it lacks in the usual charms of a *barri* (neighbourhood). There is no corner shop here for last-minute shopping or gossip, nor the bustle of a local bar. However, it is home to one of the jewels in Barcelona's crown, the Monestir de Pedralbes, a haven of peace and tranquillity and well worth visiting (*see pp120–21*).

FUNICULAR DE VALLVIDRERA

Many of the houses on the hills above Sarrià were built in the late 19th or early 20th century for the middle classes to *veranear*, or spend the hot summer months. The temperature is a few degrees cooler at these heights and it is less humid. Vallvidrera at the summit, today another 'urban village', was particularly popular. A funicular built in 1906 still provides the best possible means for getting up the hill from Peu de Funicular, the next station after Sarrià (FGC line). Until 1998 the original wooden carriages were used, adding to the charm of the journey, though the modern vehicle is reassuringly efficient, and by special request will stop halfway up in Carretera de les Aigües. This is a rough road which circumnavigates the hill, ideal for exercise and lofty views of the city.

Though not in the centre of town, the Royal Monastery of Santa María de Pedralbes is worth the short journey. This beautiful religious enclave is one of the most important buildings of Catalan Gothic. It is also a haven of peace and tranquillity and a fascinating insight on monastic life.

The monastery was founded in 1326 by Queen Elisenda de Montcada, the fourth wife of Jaume II. After his death the following year she took the order of St Clare and shut herself away here for the next 37 years. Some 20 nuns of the Order of St Clare still live near the monastery, in which they maintain an interest. They left the monastery in the early 1980s and the cells, refectory and infirmary they left behind still seem warm with life.

The monastery complex is approached through a stone portal that opens on to the gardens of the Plaça de Monestir. The church has a separate entrance beyond the monastery, and over its lintel are the arms of Elisenda, the Montcada family and the royal house of Barcelona. Queen Elisenda's tomb is set in the wall so it could be venerated both in the church and in the monastery, wearing her royal wedding dress on one side, a nun's habit the other.

The monastery is set around a cloister with a most elegant three-storey colonnade. The view of this cloister, with cypress and fruit trees and a perfect octagonal belfry, is a pinnacle of Catalan Gothic and is contemporary with the city's finest Gothic church, Santa María del Mar. Around the colonnaded cloisters are the bare cells of the nuns, with prie-dieux and small openings for food to be handed to them. The dispensary has various jars of medicines and potions, and the dining table in the refectory is laid and ready for food, which would have been grown from the vegetable gardens that can be glimpsed through the windows.

Just to the right as you arrive at the cloister is the Capella (chapel) de Sant Miguel, which has a beautiful mural of the life of Christ by the Catalan painter Ferrer Bassa, completed in 1346 for Francesca Saportella, abbess and niece of Queen Elisenda. Bassa had studied in Italy and this painting, which links Catalan Gothic to the Italian Renaissance, is the finest surviving Gothic painting in the city. To the left is the chapter house with a collection of relics and furniture from the monastery, including a model of the building.

At the far end of the cloister is the Queen's Hall and former dormitories. Until recently this was home to part of the Thyssen-Bornemisza collection which can now be seen in the Museu Nacional d'Art de Catalunya (MNAC) on Montjuïc (*see p101*).

The paintings are part of the collection built up by two generations of the Thyssen-Bornemisza family of industrialists. Though domiciled in Switzerland, Hans Heinrich, the last Baron, donated the paintings to Spain, largely through the influence of his fifth wife, Carmen 'Tita' Cervera, a former Miss Spain. The largest part of the collection, which was permanently acquired by the state in 1993, is in the Villahermosa Palace in Madrid. The monastery's own treasures are now on display.

Baixada del Monestir 9. Tel: 932 039 282. www.museuhistoria.bcn.es. Open: 10am–2pm. Closed: Mon. Admission charge. FGC: Reina Elisenda.

Opposite: The cloister of the Monastery of Pedralbes

Tibidabo and Collserola

The Collserola range of hills forms a backdrop to the city and a distinctive skyline with its high-tech communications tower and floodlit temple at the summit, Tibidabo. This is just the tip of its 8,000 hectares of parkland, Barcelona's hidden playground hardly used by most residents. Easily accessible, the area is well worth exploring for a breath of fresh air and spectacular views.

Norman Foster's communications tower

Carretera de les Aigües

This dirt track winds around the side of the hill on the city side for several kilometres, giving a bird's-eye view of the city. Overpopulated with joggers and cyclists at weekends, it is ideal for exercise and getting the city into perspective during the week.
FGC to Peu del Funicular station then funicular. Press button to request stop at Carretera de les Aigües.

Parc de Collserola

The park stretching behind the hills

Lofty views are the compensation for climbing the Collserola hills

is easily accessible from the centre of Barcelona and full of footpaths, picnic places, *merenderos* (shack-like restaurants where you can grill your own *botifarras*, Catalan sausages, or choose from the menu) and where the scent of the pine woods and the cooler air is a salvation in summer. During the week it is quiet enough to hear the birds singing and if you are lucky you may run into a family of *porc sanglars* (wild boar).

FGC train to Baixador de Vallvidrera, the first station after the tunnel through the hill, is only 13 minutes from Plaça Catalunya, and a good starting point.

Tibidabo

Legend has it that this was the hill where Christ was led by Satan to be tempted – *tibi dabo*, all this will I give you. Whether this be Catalan pride or not, there is no denying that on a clear day the view over the city and the Mediterranean from its 512m (1680ft) peak is quite spectacular. The Parc d'Atraccions and church, Temple of Sagrat Cor, at the top are less interesting but the excursion is worthwhile. Rattle up to the base of the funicular in the Tramvia Blau, a pretty blue wooden tram still going strong after 100 years of service. It passes elegant *modernista* buildings, once the summer houses of the Catalan bourgeoisie, and stops in Plaça Doctor Andreu where the funicular completes the journey to the top.

As fairgrounds go, this is more attractive than most, thanks to its retro feel which along with the view appeals to bored parents. Children love it all, especially the *montaña rusa* which seems to drop over the edge of the hillside.

Tel: 932 117 942. Open: July–Aug, Wed–Sun from 12 noon; weekends only in winter; closing times vary. Check www.tibidabo.es. FGC: Av Tibidabo. Bus: 17.

Torre de Collserola

Norman Foster's communications tower was designed for the 1992 Olympic Games, along with Santiago Calatrava's tower on Montjuïc. It is best to visit it on a clear day, and take the transparent lift to the observation platform 560m (1840ft) above sea level.

Open: Wed–Sun 11am–2.30pm, 3.30–6pm (7pm in summer). All day Sat & Sun. Combined ticket with Colom (see p54). Admission charge. Bus 211 or walk from FGC Vallvidrera Superior.

All the fun of the fair in Tibidabo plus a view

Twin towers overlook the waterfront

Vila Olímpica

Built to accommodate the hundreds of athletes who swarmed into Barcelona in July 1992, the Olympic Village was a major undertaking which completely transformed an obsolete industrial zone – a vital element in the restructuring of the city.

Before the cynical gaze of neighbouring residents it was completed, albeit at the eleventh hour, and it was the scene of much festivity during the Games. Afterwards it seemed like a ghost town – but now, over ten years later, it has an established feel: the green spaces are lush, the children's parks are well used, and it is just another neighbourhood of Barcelona.

Urban art was a feature of '90s Barcelona

Its construction involved rerouting a railway line, a whole new sewerage system and the demolition of old factories. In today's bright sunlit streets, landscaped with gardens and looking over long stretches of golden sand, it is hard to imagine that until the late 1980s it was a drab no-go area where the beaches had become a dumping ground. A few strategic chimneys remain as a reminder of its industrial past.

The most distinctive elements in the new village are the twin towers forming a gateway to the Olympic Port and the sea (*see pp34–7*). Amidst the smart yachts and smooth motor cruisers in the marina is a municipal sailing school offering courses throughout the year and yachts for charter. The port is lined with restaurants of varying standards, fast food to fresh. The main drag of the village itself is Avinguda Icària, with a 'hard park' designed by Enric Miralles running down the middle. A depressing shopping mall transports you to some unidentifiable city in the American midwest, but it does include the best cinema complex in Barcelona, the Yelmo, where 15 screens show *v.o.* (original language) films. The surrounding blocks of apartments, however, are identifiably Barcelona. In keeping with the zeal to create a striking new city, architects from around the world as well as leading Spanish and Catalan architects were involved in its construction.

Some 200 new buildings were built, all with a different design. The most desirable are along Avinguda Salvador Espriu, where the flats have a sea view and the thundering Ronda Litoral (the ring road) is covered with gardens. The inland blocks have peaceful landscaped courtyards. Of particular architectural interest are the Eurocity buildings on the crossroads of Icària and Rosa Sensat by local architects Piñon and Vilaplana, and the Telefónica building on Icària by

Jaume Bach and Gabriel Mora. Property prices here are inaccessible to the average person, making it a privileged residential area. But it has taken off as a playground for Barcelonans with rollerbladers, cyclists and skateboarders cruising along the front, swarms of promenading families and hordes of sun worshippers on the beaches, and a different crowd by night. The Vila Olímpica now merges with neighbouring Poble Nou as an established part of the city, while the newly built Diagonal Mar has the feel of a new town still surrounded by cranes as development continues.

The twin towers are the gateway between Olympic Village and Olympic Port

The combination of post-Franco energy and Barcelona winning its bid for the XXV Olympiad made for a high-octane mix in the 1980s and early 1990s. Nowhere was this so clearly manifested as in the world of architecture. A lot of new building had to be achieved in record time, old buildings had to be renovated, and a huge urban renewal scheme had already begun.

Young architects were given the opportunity of a lifetime, and with due flair the challenge was taken up. International architects were also brought in. As well as the key Olympic buildings (*see pp90–93 and 124–5*), there are many other projects which merit attention.

One such project came out of Oriol Bohigas' new urban design department in the City Council. Disparagingly known as 'hard parks', they were more positively 'urban spaces' which in a city second only to Calcutta in density was a welcome prospect. Young architects came up with creative design solutions for making public spaces out of dark alleyways or abandoned land. One of the earliest examples was the Parc de l'Escorxador near Plaça Espanya, also known as the Parc de Joan Miró after his distinctive tall sculpture, *Woman and Bird*. Nearby is the famous Plaça dels Països Catalans by Viaplana, Piñon and Miralles who were to become star architects over the following years. Parc de la Creueta del Coll was built in a quarry, providing the neglected neighbourhood with a much-appreciated lake to swim in.

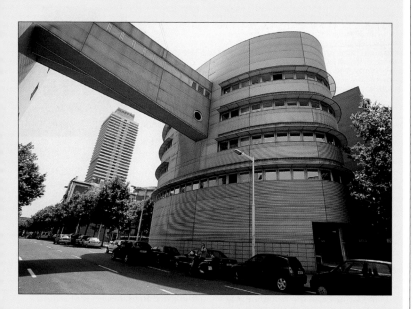

A second wave of architecture followed in 1992. The Teatre Nacional, designed by Ricardo Bofill, was built near Plaça de les Glòries, followed a few years later by Rafael Moneo's concert hall, L'Auditori. Much of this second wave has been about urban renewal. Richard Meier's Contemporary Art Museum in the Raval was a vital piece in opening up this forsaken area. More recently the Rambla del Raval has opened, a new urban space letting light into a dark, dense neighbourhood.

The third wave has come with the new century, focusing on the Forum 2004 and the Diagonal Mar (see pp58–9). This is based on worthy principles of creating a new residential area and building a sustainable city, but the increasing demand for hotels and office space has provoked speculation on a large scale. Recent projects seem to be more geared towards commercialism than urban renewal. Bohigas was horrified by the World Trade Center, blocking the city's new view of the sea. The old bullring in Plaça Espanya is to become yet another commercial centre. It is to be hoped that some projects will straddle both camps, like the hotel and film theatre complex on the Rambla del Raval. Will it bring life and trade into a neglected area, or will it just alienate in an area short of public housing?

Opposite: Calatrava's Bac de Roda bridge
Above: Bach and Mora's striking building in the Olympic Village

Zona Universitaria

At the extreme end of Avinguda Diagonal, its furthest point from the sea, is one of the main entrances to Barcelona, bringing traffic from Madrid and Lleida. A confusion of slip roads and junctions suddenly clears to reveal the long straight avenue plunging down towards the Eixample and the city centre. As the name suggests, this area is dominated by the university campus.

Faculty of Arts, Barcelona University

What to some appears to be a no-man's land scattered with high-rise buildings is to others the beginning of an open-air museum, where several generations of architects have left their showpieces. Two of the latest buildings are the Hotel Rey Juan Carlos I and the neighbouring Palau de Congressos de Catalunya, both by local architect Carles Ferrater. The hotel accommodates the many delegates who now flood into Barcelona for

University buildings

conferences, and it is favoured by the Spanish royal family as well as world politicians for its capacity to be cordoned off. Its spacious gardens and lake were annexed from a beautiful old house, Torre Melina, which was demolished to make way for the hotel.

Bordering the other side of the avenue is the Parc de Cervantes, known for its roses, notably the off-white Barcelona rose. Opposite the park is an exclusive tennis club, the Reial Club Tennis Turó. Many of its members, like those of the nearby Polo Club, are typical residents of this area, a different world from downtown Barcelona.

The University of Barcelona began to expand into this area from its central headquarters in the 1950s, a plan which was accelerated by student unrest provoked by the Franco regime. The Faculty of Law, at No 684, was built in record time using prefabricated material to house the unruly young lawyers. It is considered the best example of the International Style in the city and stands out as a rarity, as modern architecture was being repressed by Madrid at the time.

Oriol Bohigas, instrumental architect in Olympic Barcelona, describes it as the city's 'first civilized modern public building' after the Civil War. In recent times the university site has expanded, with the new UPC (Polytechnic University of Catalonia) opening its southern campus here.

As the university faculties begin to merge with the domineering commercial buildings which continue to line the avenue as far as Plaça Francesc Macià there is a refreshing green space: the gardens of the royal palace, Palau de Pedralbes (*see pp130–31*), a welcoming haven of peace. From here the stream of students flows into the brisk march of

office workers, a perfect illustration of the Catalan work ethic. The mood only lightens when there is a Barça match in the Camp Nou stadium tucked in behind this part of the Diagonal. Then the crowds pour into the metro stations and towards their cars parked for miles around this area. Whether jubilant or depressed (in the dramatic way Barça supporters feel their team's losses), they are a colourful bunch. Lone pensioners, grandparents and grandchildren, fathers and daughters (and the boyfriend), foreign students, boisterous lads, the wide gamut of Barça devotees provides a refreshing injection of life into this commercial and financial district.

A mecca for football fans everywhere, Camp Nou

Walk: Palau Reial de Pedralbes and Pabellons Güell

More of a meander than a walk, this gentle route visits a 20th-century royal palace, a couple of museums, some ornamental gardens and a lesser-known Gaudí site, all within an estate that used to belong to the Güell family. *Allow 1–2 hours.*

Take the metro (line 3) to Palau Reial, or try the luxury Tomb bus, an exclusive service that runs from Plaça Catalunya to Plaça Pius XII, with suede seats and elegant señoras. More expensive than the normal bus but much more comfortable, and cheaper than a taxi.

All sights on this walk are within the Parc del Palau Reial de Pedralbes.

1 Jardins del Palau Reial de Pedralbes

This public park in the grounds of the royal palace is peaceful and serene after the busy commercial Avinguda Diagonal. Its central part is laid out as an ornamental garden, and its gravel paths are a favourite for wedding photographs. The land used to be part of an estate owned by the Güell family, ceded by the son of Eusebi Güell for the construction of the palace. Wander off the beaten track and you may find the small fountain-cum-bench designed by Gaudí before 1884, which was rediscovered after 100 years of being overgrown with ivy.

2 Palau Reial de Pedralbes

The attractive palace is not as historic as it looks. It is the result of a conversion of one of the houses on the estate, Can Feliu, which with the agreement of the people of Barcelona was given to the king Alfonso XIII when he came to visit. It is occasionally used for state banquets but not open to the public, except for the wings housing the two museums.

3 Museu de Ceràmica and Museu de les Arts Decoratives

Located in the wings of the palace are these two small but interesting museums. The Ceramic Museum follows the history of Spanish pottery from the 11th century to the present, including some Miró and Picasso pieces. The Decorative Arts Museum looks at the design of everyday objects from medieval times until today. They both hold temporary exhibitions.

*Av Diagonal 686. Tel: 932 801 621
(Ceramic); 932 805 024 (Decorative Arts).
Open: Tue–Sat 10am–6pm, Sun
10am–3pm. Admission free on first Sun
of month.*
*Leave the gardens and turn left down
Diagonal to Plaça Pius XII, then left into
the broad Avinguda Pedralbes, which goes
up to the monastery (see pp120–21).*

4 Facultat de Dret

On the corner is the Faculty of Law, one
of the many university buildings in this
upper part of Diagonal. Built in 1958, it
is regarded as the best example of the
International Style in Barcelona (*see
pp128–9*).

5 Pabellons de la Finca Güell

One of the few Gaudí works you can see
without the usual crush, being relatively
far from the centre. This was the
entrance to the Güell estate and consists
of lodge houses and stables behind.
The extraordinary gate is a sculpted
dragon, an important mythical beast in
Catalan culture. Recently opened to the
public, the pavilions are one of the
centres for the Ruta del Modernisme,
or do-it-yourself tour of *modernista*
buildings.
*Avinguda de Pedralbes 15, corner of
George R Collins (street recently named
after the American historian who
promoted Gaudí's fame in the 1950s).*

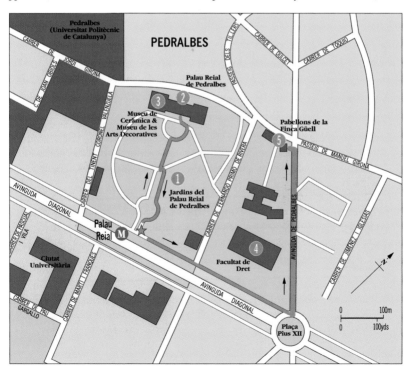

In May 1992, Ronald Koeman's penalty kick that netted the coveted European Cup for FC Barcelona for the first time in its history plunged all Catalonia into days of euphoric celebration. Since arch-rivals Real Madrid had already won the cup six times, nothing that Barcelona's celebrated Olympic Games were to bring would ever match that moment.

The slogan that has been repeated ad nauseam is true: 'Barça és més qu'un club'. Barça is more than a club, more than a city football team: it is a national institution, a way of life. It draws supporters from the whole of Catalonia, and Catalan communities across the world have their barcelonista circles.

One of the oldest clubs in Europe, it was founded in 1899 and soon became well established. It always seemed, though, that the dice were heavily loaded in favour of Real Madrid, an organ of the central government. Barça's history is filled with incidents that show that this rivalry went far deeper than sport: it was a political issue. In one notorious episode, when Barcelona signed the brilliant player Kubala in 1951, their fortunes improved considerably and the team became so powerful that the Spanish government forced the removal of the equally brilliant DiStefano and dictated that he play for Real Madrid.

During the repressive Franco years, the team functioned as 'the army of Catalonia', for Barça was the only outlet for the collective expression of Catalan national identity. The Catalan flag was banned, and so the *blaugrana* (blue and garnet) flag took on huge significance. It was instrumental in integrating the huge numbers of immigrants from southern Spain and elsewhere, uniting them with the 'born and bred' Catalans in a common cause. Barça's vicissitudes are still followed with almost religious fervour, and victories are greeted with fireworks, partying crowds on the Rambla and honking horns.

Barça has strong roots in Catalan society. The club has over 100,000 members, most of whom have permanent seats, with membership passing from parent to child. Visitors can look around the fabulous Camp Nou Stadium and take in the FC Barcelona Museum (the city's second most visited one after the Picasso) which contains a blow-by-blow history of the club with audiovisuals, glittering trophies and an assortment of boots, shirts, photos, referees' whistles and other paraphernalia (*see p136*).

Barça also fields basketball, handball, ice hockey and roller hockey teams, with smaller though equally devoted followings. The winning of the European Cup by the basketball team in 2003 triggered ecstatic celebrations to equal any football triumphs.

Opposite page and above: Memorabilia in the 'Barça' museum

Many museum buildings
are worth visiting in
themselves

Museums

There are 68 museums in Barcelona, innumerable art galleries and several cultural centres run by local authorities and private organisations. Avoiding some of the more obscure, like the Museum of Horse-Drawn Hearses or the Museum of Dentistry, this list has been reduced to the most popular and best organised and includes the major cultural centres known for their high standard of exhibitions. Art galleries are all over town, but special concentrations of them are in Consell de Cent, near Passeig de Gràcia, and in the Old Town, the more avant-garde being in the Born and Raval neighbourhoods.

Caixa Forum

Fascinating *modernista* textile factory restored into 'la Caixa' Foundation's stimulating cultural centre, where their contemporary art collection, one of the largest in Europe, can be displayed. Music festivals, family activities, temporary exhibitions, conferences and media library are all available here. *Nits d'estiu* is a special programme of night-time events for summer evenings. (*See also pp98 and 100.*)
Av Marquès de Comillas 6–8. Tel: 902 223 040. www.fundacio.lacaixa.es. Open: Tue–Sun 10am–8pm. Closed: Mon. Free admission. Metro: Espanya.

Centre Cultural Caixa Catalunya (La Pedrera)

Gaudí's apartment block the Casa Milà, or La Pedrera, is owned by the Caixa Catalunya and used as their cultural centre. Apart from the Espai Gaudí, a useful exhibition of his work, and

El Pis, the show flat, there is space on the first floor with high-quality temporary exhibitions free of charge. *Provença 261. Tel: 902 400 973. www.caixacatalunya.es. Open: daily 10am–8pm. Admission charge (to Espai and El Pis/roof terrace). Metro: Diagonal. FGC: Provença.*

Fundació Antoni Tàpies

Comprehensive collection of one of Catalonia's and Spain's greatest living artists, Antoni Tàpies, mostly donated by the artist himself. Shows the evolution of his work.
Aragó 255. Tel: 934 870 315. www.fundaciotapies.org. Open: Tue–Sun 10am–8pm. Closed: Mon. Admission charge. Metro: Passeig de Gràcia.

Fundació Joan Miró

Large collection of Miró's work from 1914 to 1978, including paintings, sculptures, drawing and textiles. Also

houses the Mercury fountain designed by Alexander Calder for the Spanish Republican pavilion in the 1937 Paris Exhibition. Holds an annual festival of contemporary music.
Av Miramar 1. Tel: 934 439 470. www.bcn.fjmiro.es. Open: Tue–Sat 10am–7pm, Thur 10am–9.30pm, Sun 10am–2.30pm. Closed: Mon. Admission charge. Metro: Paral.lel + Funicular. Bus: 50, 55.

Museu d'Art Contemporani de Barcelona (MACBA)
A striking building houses the contemporary art collection that is almost more about urban renewal programmes than art (*see p50*). Its collection covers the period from the 1950s to the present.
Plaça dels Angels 1. Tel: 934 120 810. www.macba.es. Open: 11am–7.30pm, Sat 10am–8pm, Sun 10am–3pm. Closed: Tue. Admission charge. Metro: Catalunya or Universitat. FGC: Catalunya.

Museu de Cera
The wax museum near the end of La Rambla is amusing for children on a rainy day.
Pasatge Banca 5–7. Tel: 933 172 649. www.museocerabcn.com. Open: Mon–Fri 10am–1.30pm, 4–7.30pm; Sat–Sun 11am–2pm, 4.30–8.30pm. Daily until 10pm in summer. Admission charge. Metro: Drassanes. Bus: 14, 59, 64.

CosmoCaixa
Owned by the prosperous 'la Caixa' Foundation, this excellent science museum at the foot of Tibidabo has recently reopened after major extensions to its *modernista* premises. Improvements have made it one of the best of the new generation of science museums. Whether it's immersing yourself in the 1,000sq m of Amazon forest, bugs and all, or observing the wonders of the universe in the Planetarium, this museum is entertaining and stimulating for the whole family. There is even an area for 3–6-year-olds, the ingenious Clik dels Nens.
Teodor Roviralta, 47–51. Tel: 932 126 050. www.cosmocaixa.com. Open: Tue–Sun 10am–8pm. Admission charge. FGC: Av Tibidabo.

Museu d'Història de Catalunya
The museum of Catalonia's history works as a generic history museum as well and is interesting for all the family. Try on a medieval knight's armour, build a Roman arch, there is plenty to do. Housed in a stylishly renovated warehouse on the harbour.
Plaça Pau Vila 3. Tel: 932 254 700. cultura.gencat.net/mhc. Open: Tue–Sat

The perfect setting for Miró's work

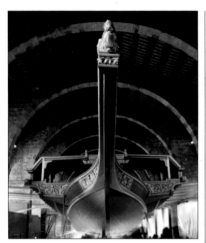

Exhibit at the Museu Marítim

10am–7pm, Sun 10am–2.30pm. Closed:
Mon. Admission charge. Metro:
Barceloneta. Bus: 14, 17, 59, 64.

Museu d'Història de la Ciutat

Fascinating insight into the history of
Barcelona, including an underground
visit to 4,000sq m (43,000sq ft) of
archaeological remains beneath the
square and the cathedral, from 1 BC
to AD 9. You can also climb to the top
of a 16th-century watchtower.
Plaça del Rei. Tel: 933 151 111.
www.museuhistoria.bcn.es. Open:
Tue–Sat 10am–8pm, Sun 10am–3pm.
Oct–May closed at lunchtime. Closed:
Mon. Admission charge. Metro: Jaume I,
Liceu or Catalunya. Bus: 16, 17, 40, 45.

Museu Futbol Club Barcelona President Nuñez

An essential for football fans, this
museum of Barça paraphernalia
includes a spectacular view of the
stadium, and a chance to skate on
the ice-skating rink. (See pp132–3.)
Aristides Maillol 12–18. Enter through
gates 7 or 9. Tel: 934 963 600.
www.fcbarcelona.com. Open: Mon–Sat
10am–6.30pm, Sun 10am–2pm. Closed
when a match is on. Admission charge.
Metro: Collblanc. Bus: 15, 52, 53, 54.

Museu Marítim

The maritime museum has recently
been refurbished to include a space for
temporary exhibitions, and to show
more of these impressive medieval
shipyards (see p54). Part of the museum
is afloat on the quayside nearby: in the
1918 sailing boat Santa Eulàlia, which
can be boarded.
Av Drassanes 1. Tel: 933 429 920.
www.diba.es/mmaritim. Open: daily
10am–7pm. Admission charge. Metro:
Drassanes. Bus: 14, 18, 59, 64.

Museu Nacional d'Art de Catalunya (MNAC)

Reopened in December 2004 after
extensive renovation by Italian
architect Gae Aulenti, the Palau
Nacional on Montjuïc now houses 1,000
years of art. Its prized Romanesque
collection, one of the best in the world,
and Gothic and Renaissance pieces have
now been complemented by the 19th-
and 20th-century pieces formerly
housed in the Modern Art Museum in
the Parc de la Ciutadella. There are also
photographic and numismatic items,
and a part of Spain's Thyssen-
Bornemisza collection (see p101).
Originally built for the 1929 Exposition,
this monumental building offers
splendid vistas of the city. The 19th- and

20th-century collection covers the work of artists who were in the same circle as Picasso, notably Casas, Nonell and Rusiñol, and includes *modernista* furniture and graphics. The Thyssen-Bornemisza collection has pieces by Fra Angelico, Tiziano, Zurbarán and Canaletto amongst others. The MNAC also holds good temporary exhibitions.
Palau Nacional, Parc de Montjuïc. Tel: 936 220 375. www.mnac.es. Open: Tue–Sat 10am–7pm, Sun 10am–2.30pm. Admission charge. Metro: Espanya. Bus: 50, 55.

Museu Picasso

The most-visited museum in Barcelona and one of the most attractive. Spread across five medieval palaces, it contains the largest collection in the world of the artist's formative years, as well as some from the Blue Period and the famous studies of *Las Meninas*.
Montcada 15–23. Tel: 933 196 310. www.museupicasso.bcn.es. Open: Tue–Sun 10am–8pm. Closed: Mon. Admission charge. Metro: Jaume I. Bus: 14, 17, 36, 64.

Museu Tèxtil i d'Indumentària

Housed in one of the many palaces in this medieval street, the textile museum has a small but attractive collection. The café in its courtyard and shop are both worth a pause.
Montcada 12–14. Tel: 933 197 603. www.museutextil.bcn.es. Open: Tue–Sat 10am–6pm, Sun 10am–3pm. Closed: Mon. Admission charge. Metro: Jaume I. Bus: 14, 17, 36, 64.

The MACBA, Museum of Contemporary Art, in the Raval district

Getting Away From It All

Golden beaches, sturdy castles, wine houses, wetlands, medieval towns and modern resorts are all easily accessible, and help visitors get a feel for the region from which Barcelona has grown. From Dalí's eccentricities in the north to Port Aventura in the south, there is something for everyone to enjoy.

A quiet square in Girona

CISTERCIAN ROUTE (LA RUTA DEL CISTER)

A triangle of handsome Cistercian monasteries lies just inland from Tarragona among vineyards, almond and olive groves. Founded in the wake of the Counts of Barcelona as they took southern (or 'New') Catalonia from the Moors in the 12th century, they are havens of peace and tranquillity. Ideally reached by car, but check with the local tourist office for current tours.

Monestir de Poblet

Grandest of them all is the Monestir de Poblet, which also served as a royal palace and pantheon. Set in tranquil countryside 10km (6 miles) from Montblanc, its golden stones hide a complete community of buildings that make it the largest inhabited monastery in Europe. It is now a UNESCO World Heritage Site with 180,000 visitors a year. Like most Catalan religious houses, it has been severely set upon in its time: by the French in the War of Independence and by locals in the 19th-century Carlist Wars.
Tel: 977 871 247. Open daily. Admission charge.

Monestir de Santes Creus

The church in this monastery, nearest to Tarragona by the village of Valls, is a perfect example of Cistercian architecture, though it was not completed until the 18th century. It has the tomb of Jaume II (1291–1327) and its cloisters show the first sign of Gothic in Catalan. It is the only one of the three not to be used by a religious order, and its rooms are therefore more accessible.
Tel: 977 638 329. Open daily, except Mon. Tue free.

Vallbona de Les Monges

The smallest of the three and the only one in a village, which has the same name. It has been in continuous occupation by Cistercian nuns since 1157, and contains the tomb of Violant of Hungary, Jaume I's queen.
Tel: 973 330 266. Open daily, except Mon & Sun mornings.

COSTA BRAVA

The Costa Brava, the 'wild coast', is one of the most attractive in the Mediterranean, with pine-backed coves, soaring cliffs and sandy beaches. It begins at **Blanes**, where the terrain forces the railway from Barcelona inland, and continues north to the French border 67km (42 miles) away. Trains run to Blanes, Girona and Figueres, where there are bus connections to the rest of the coast. Hiring a car for a day or two is another option.

The major resorts are **Lloret de Mar**, **Tossa de Mar** and **Platja D'Aro**, all with good beaches and plenty of hotels. More intimate are the resorts and coves around **Palafrugell**, such as **Calella**, **Llafranc**, **Tamariu** and **Aiguablava** where there is a Parador and the Hotel Aiguablava, the most famous on the coast. Just inland are the historic medieval towns of **Pals** and **Peratalada**, good places to stop for lunch.

The biggest expanse of beach is the golden scimitar of the **Bay of Roses**. This is where the Greeks and Romans first set foot in Spain, at **Empúries**, and the remains of their 'emporium', with the Greek harbour wall, can be visited, as can the Iberian settlement of **Ullastret** near Pals.

At the top of the bay is the resort of **Roses** and Ferran Adrià's three-Michelin-star **El Bulli**, voted by *Restaurant Magazine* as the best restaurant in the world.
Cala Montjoi, Roses. Tel: 972 150 457. www.elbulli.com. Open: Apr–Sept.

Roses is on the last folds of the Pyrenees. Just beyond, over a zigzag mountain road, is Spain's most easterly town, **Cadaqués**, the St Tropez of Spain in the 1960s and still with a wealthy, hippy air. It has also become synonymous with Salvador Dalí.
www.costabrava.org

The Teatro–Museu Dalí in Figueres

DALÍ COUNTRY

The three Dalí museums lie around the Empordà plain beneath the Pyrenees. The main market town of **Figueres** is a couple of hours from Barcelona by RENFE train (Plaça de Catalunya). There are bus connections to the other Dalí haunts, though a hire car may be more convenient.

Teatro–Museu Dalí

Dalí (*see pp144–5*) was born in Figueres and in 2003 the council bought the house of his birth, Carrer Monturiol 6, with a view to making it a museum. But it is his own museum in a former theatre that attracts most visitors to the town. Not all the works on display are his own, but most of the jokes are (do not miss the Mae West Room or the Rainy Cadillac), and so is the whole concept of the bread-roll plastered building. He is buried here and it is a fitting monument.
Tel: 972 677 500. www.salvador-dali.org. Open daily: 9am–7.15pm. Oct–June 10.30am–5.15pm. Closed: Mon. Admission charge.

Casa–Museu Salvador Dalí

Dalí and his wife Gala spent most of their time in Portlligat on the coast just outside Cadaqués, and their former home is a delightful museum, the Casa–Museu Salvador Dalí, reached by a tourist train from Cadaqués. Evolved from two fishermen's cottages in this unspoilt bay, it is an enchanting place, proving he may have been a better interior designer than a painter. There are many small touches, such as the bed positioned to make him the first person in Spain to see the sun rise each day.

Tel: 972 251 015. www.salvador-dali.org. Open daily: 10.30am–9pm. Closed: Mon, Oct–Mar and from Jan–mid-Mar. Tickets should be reserved 1–2 days in advance.

Casa–Museu Castell Gala Dalí

At Púbol 40km (25 miles) from Figueres, Dalí's 'gift to Gala' once again shows his great taste and flair for interiors, with some of his work on the walls of this three-storey 14th-century castle, which he restored. A collection of Gala's 'gala' dresses is also on permanent exhibition. She lived here on and off from 1971, when they bought it, and she is buried here. Dalí moved in after her death before his last years spent in the tower of his museum in Figueres.

Tel: 972 488 655. www.salvador-dali.org. Open daily: 10.30am–8pm. Closed: Mon, Sept–Mar and from Nov–mid-Mar. The castle is 4km (2½ miles) from Flaça station on the Figueres line. A bus stop at Flaça is 2km (1 mile) from Púbol.

GIRONA

Girona is a Barcelona in the provinces and a day can easily be passed exploring its calm museums and shady medieval streets. Trains leave regularly from Plaça Catalunya in Barcelona and take about an hour.

From the carp-filled River Onyar, Girona's old town rises above earth-coloured waterfront houses. A stone bridge beside them leads to the attractive **Rambla** and the start of the old town. Through its heart is Via Augusta, the Roman road that ran from Rome, through France and down to Tarragona (*see pp142–3*). Behind this ancient lane is the Jewish Quarter or Call, now the **Centre Bonastruc Ça Porta**. This was home to several hundred Jews from the late 9th century until their expulsion in 1492.

Approached through the door in an alley, Carrer de Sant Llorenç, which

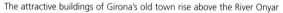

The attractive buildings of Girona's old town rise above the River Onyar

was the only entrance to the quarter, it is open every day and is a centre of research and learning.

Via Augusta leaves the town under an arch where the Angel of Good Death looked down on those taken from the city to be hanged. Just before the arch a magnificent flight of steps rises to the imposing **cathedral**, pure Catalan Gothic, with the widest nave in Christendom. Its museum contains some beautiful artefacts, including *The Creation*, a stunning 11th-century tapestry. In the neighbouring former Episcopal Palace is the **Museu d'Art**, with a rich collection of Romanesque and Gothic church art.

The city museum, the **Museu d'Història de la Ciutat**, is in a former Capuchin convent, with a display of instruments showing the evolution of *sardana* music. Across the river in the new town is the **Museu del Cinema** (*Carrer Sequia 1*), with exhibits going back to the 19th century.

To get a good view of the town take the **Passeig Archaeològic** behind the cathedral, which runs along the top of the medieval walls. Catalunya Bus Turístic offers day trips to Girona and Figueres from Barcelona. *Tel: 932 853 832.*

MONTSERRAT

The holy high spot for Catalan Christians is the mountain of Montserrat and the monastery where its famous choir sings twice a day. The FGC train from Plaça Espanya to Aeri de Montserrat takes an hour and from there a cable car or zip train completes the journey.

Montserrat ('serrated mountain') is a truly rugged outcrop of dozens of rocky fingers poking up to 1,236m (4,055ft). Scattered over it are chapels and hermits' caves, but at its centre is a monastery and basilica where **La Moreneta**, the Black Virgin of Montserrat, patroness of Catalonia, is venerated.

Although the monastery dates from the 9th century, today's buildings are disappointingly modern, as the whole place was destroyed by the French in 1811 when Napoleon's forces hunted down the monks and hermits 'like goats'. Nevertheless, the sheer setting of the place, rebuilt and repopulated by Benedictine monks in 1844, remains dramatic.

La Moreneta stands behind the altar protected by glass, and pilgrims come to touch her orb. She is reputed to have been made by St Luke, brought here by St Peter in AD 50, and later hidden in a cave (the **Santa Cova**, which can be visited via a funicular railway, as can the hermitage of St John). Modern science says that she dates from the 12th century.

Montserrat, the Holy Mountain, where Catalan Christians come to touch the black Madonna

There are shops, cafés and a hotel in the complex. A museum has paintings, relics and liturgical items. Try to get here in time to hear the monastery hymn, *Virolai*, at 1pm. *Salve Regina* is sung at 7.10pm. The choir takes a break in July and over the Christmas period. A CD is a suitable souvenir.
Tel: 938 777 701. Open daily.

PORT AVENTURA
Just south of Tarragona near the resort of **Salou** is Port Aventura, one of the biggest adventure theme parks in Europe, which will keep children amused and spending money all day. Run by Universal Studios, it stretches across more than 1sq km of elaborate scenery re-creating five areas from around the world. These are the Great Wall of China, with what is claimed to be the biggest roller coaster ride in continental Europe, a Polynesian paradise, ruins of Mayan Mexico, a Mediterranean idyll and the Wild West where cowboys enact an *estampida*.
Tel: 977 779 000. www.portaventura.es. Open daily. Closed: mid-Jan–mid-Mar. Port Aventura has its own railway station, reached from Barcelona via Tarragona. One hour by car.

SITGES
For a taste of the seaside beyond Barcelona, head for Sitges, 35km (22 miles) south of the city and easily reached by train from Passeig de Gràcia or Sants. It has been popular with Barcelonans for nearly two centuries, and it remains elegant, exuberant and relaxed, with clean, golden beaches, excellent restaurants and numerous lively bars. It also has a flourishing gay population which dominates the outrageous annual pre-Lent carnival.

The pretty fishing village was taken up by 19th-century artists, whose use of blues and pinks gave them the name of Luminists, and it was Santiago Rusiñol (1861–1931), a founder of the *modernista* Quatre Gats café in Barcelona, who put the town on the art map when he bought an El Greco painting and paraded it through the streets to his house, now the **Museu Cau Ferrat**. Sited above the sea, it has an intriguing collection of paintings, ceramics and ironwork. Opposite is the **Museu Maricel**, another lovely building, with murals by Josep Maria Sert. There is also a **Museu Romàntic** in the town, which has been restored with a 19th-century domestic interior.

TARRAGONA
When the Romans conquered the Iberian peninsula they divided it into three provinces. The Eastern one was Tarraconensis (Tarragona), and it is the best place in Catalonia to see Roman remains. Trains run directly from Barcelona and take about two hours.

One of the beaches at Sitges, a popular place for Barcelonans to go for Sunday lunch

The Rambla in Tarragona comes to a dead halt above the sea, which gives it the name of 'the balcony of Europe'. From here you can look down on the Roman **amphitheatre**, still largely intact. Behind it is the **Museu Nacional Arqueològic**, which has a large collection of Roman artefacts. But to feel the might of the Roman empire, walk along the kilometre that remains of the Roman wall, built of stones of such size it is hard to know how it was possible to cut and place them here. The Gothic **cathedral** with a tranquil cloister of orange trees is also worth visiting. A steep hill leads down to the Serallo part of the old port, and here there are excellent fish restaurants where a meal can be washed down with Tarragona's fine wine.

VIC

The best time to visit this inland town is market day, Tuesday or Saturday, when stalls fill the unusually large, arcaded main square and rural characters crowd the streets. Here you can buy the town's speciality, a salami called *fuet*.

The **cathedral**, remodelled in a neoclassical style in the 19th century, has a grand Romanesque tower, and murals painted by Josep Maria Sert (who decorated the Rockefeller Center in New York). Enormous figures from the Bible form theatrical tableaux on the walls, which he painted twice: the first attempt did not survive the Civil War. Sert is buried in the 14th-century cloister. The adjoining **Museu Episcopal** has the finest collection of Romanesque art outside Barcelona. The town has an atmospheric medieval Plaça Major.

WINE ROUTE

The wines of Catalonia are some of the most interesting in Spain (*see p165*). A speciality is *cava*, a Champagne-method wine, and the heart of its production is **Sant Sadurní d'Anoia**, 45 minutes by train from Plaça de Catalunya. The house of Freixenet produces some 80 per cent of Catalunya's *cava* and there are tours regularly throughout the day. *Tel: 938 917 000.*

Codorníu, the house that 'invented' *cava*, has a beautiful *modernista* factory, with a museum of posters and related graphic art, as well as tours. *Tel: 938 183 232.*

Nearby **Vilafranca del Penedès** is the centre for still wine and a **Museu del Vi** is housed in the 14th-century royal palace. *Open: 10am–2pm & 4–7pm, Sun 10am–2pm. Closed: Mon. Admission charge.* The tourist office gives details of all the bodegas and producers that can be visited in the area. *Tel: 938 920 358.*

WETLAND WILDLIFE

The **Parc Natural del Delta d'Ebre** covers 70sq km (27sq miles) at the mouth of Spain's longest river, the Ebre. This nature reserve is one of the most important wildlife habitats in Europe. It is best to visit by car, perhaps combining it with a visit to Tarragona or Port Aventura. Get your bearings in the Eco-Museu in Deltebre, and follow the recommended routes.

The marshlands at **Empúria-brava** on the Costa Brava are also an important wildlife site, and you might see flamingos, black-winged stilts, egrets and herons.

Salvador Dalí i Domènech was born in 1904 in Figueres, the market town of the Alt Empordà, where his father was a notary. For their holidays the family visited the coast at Cadaqués 25km (16 miles) away, and the two places remained with him all his life. In particular the rocky coast around Cap de Creus can be seen in many of his paintings.

In 1921 he went to the Escuela de Belles Artes in Madrid where he befriended two other students, Spain's great 20th-century poet Federico Garcia Lorca and Luis Buñuel, with whom he would make the two most famous Surrealist films, *Le Chien Andalou* (1928) and *L'Age d'Or* (1930).

With encouragement from both Picasso and Miró, Dalí went to Paris to seek his fame and fortune and it was here that, in 1929, he met André Breton and joined the Surrealists. Five years later he was famously ejected from the group, wearing a diver's helmet and several jerseys for the occasion. Surrealism looked to the subconscious and the works of Sigmund Freud, though after the father of psychiatry met Dalí he pronounced him 'a typical Spaniard – totally mad'. Dalí invented for himself the 'paranoiac-critical method' of looking at the world.

The same year that he joined the Surrealists he met Gala, the Russian wife of the French poet Paul Eluard, and they remained together for the rest of their lives. In 1930 he found and bought the fisherman's cottage at Portlligat, his home for the next 50 years. At the start of the Civil War he left for America, making his name (and the name Breton conjured for him from an anagram – *avida dollars*) with paintings, sculptures, lithographs and designs. He returned to Portlligat in 1948, having stated, to the fury of his artistic peers, that Franco had 'saved Spain'.

During the 1960s his hallucinatory images struck a chord with dreamy hippies and Cadaqués soon became the

trendiest place in Spain. Rumours of the goings-on in Dalí's Portlligat house were rampant. In 1974, with the assistance of the local authorities, he turned the run-down local theatre in Figueres into a museum, and when it opened it met with instant success.

His work tailed off in later years, and there were rumours that, as a final Surrealist joke, he had signed many blank canvases. His whole life was as much about art as his paintings, his public appearances always something of an event. In the end, after the death of Gala (whose body he failed to eat, as promised), he shut himself away in the tower of his museum in Figueres, which became his mausoleum on his death in 1989.

The Fundació Gala–Salvador, which was set up six years before his death, has been active in promoting his works in Spain and around the world. In its trust are more than 4,000 artworks and one of its patrons is Princess Cristina of Spain.

Opposite and above: Views of the Dalí Museum in Figueres, where the artist is buried

S h o p p i n g

Leading design store Vinçon once bore the logo 'I shop
therefore I am' on its perennially stylish carrier bags. To see
the crowds massing in the main shopping streets around
Plaça Catalunya on Saturdays and tourists returning home
laden with extra bags suggests it is a universal philosophy.
At least in Barcelona shopping sprees can be relieved by a
drink on a terrace or an occasional tapa.

Everything is available in
El Corte Inglés

What to buy
The unrelenting march of globalisation
has inevitably reduced the differences,
so international chains are beginning to
proliferate here and Catalan or Spanish
labels are more available elsewhere in
the world. However, there is more choice
here of national brands, and at more
affordable prices, and for the moment the
smaller businesses are just holding their
own. So you can find the corner shops
in most districts still selling their own
specialities, be it food, hardware, fans,
wickerwork or even lightning conductors.
The Old Town, Gràcia and parts of the
Eixample are best for these finds.

Ceramics
A speciality of the region, cheap,
colourful and very practical in a kitchen.
Heavy to carry home but well worth it.
The brown cooking pots, *cassoles*, can be
found in supermarkets and hardware
stores as well as the ceramic shops.

La Caixa de Fang
Wide, attractive range of pots including
some from other parts of Spain. Their
olive-wood cooking utensils are a

lighter gift alternative.
Freneria 1.

Design
A recurrent theme in Barcelona (*see
pp70–71*). A Gaudí chair may not fit in
your luggage but an oil decanter would,
or a Santa & Cole lamp.

Bd Ediciones de Diseño
Best of 20th-century and contemporary
design in an exquisite space.
Mallorca 291.

Pilma
Stylish home design including suitcases
and jewellery.
Av Diagonal 403.

Vinçon
No self-respecting designer home in
Barcelona would be without something
from here.
Passeig de Gràcia 96.

Fashion
Internationally known local designers
tend to have shops in the Eixample,
though the Born district in the

Old Town is becoming a centre for fashion.

Adolfo Dominguez
The Galician who made crushed linen fashionable is one of Spain's best-known designers. For men and women.
Passeig de Gràcia 32 and other branches.

Antonio Miró
Still a leader in Catalan fashion. Toni Miró's clothes for men and women are understated and stylish.
Consell de Cent 349.

Cannibal
In an ancient candle shop. Valenciana Angeles Salvador's easy-to-wear original clothes in wonderful materials, for men and women.
Carme 5.

David Valls
Cool, comfortable styles from this Catalan whose medium is knitwear.
València 235.

Instinto
Individual designs for women in appealing colours and comfortable styles, at an accessible price.
Banys Nous 5.

Jean Pierre Bua
Intimate shop with good atmosphere, yet it has the widest range of international labels you will find in Barcelona.
Diagonal 469.

The lesser-known designers have small boutiques, especially in the Old Town.

High-street fashion at accessible prices is everywhere. Best streets are Pelai, Portaferrisa, Portal del Angel or the large shopping centres. **Zara** (*at least nine branches in Barcelona*) is the Spanish fashion phenomenon of the century, with high turnover and effective, cheap fashion for men, women and children. An offshoot of the empire targeted at teenagers is **Bershka** (*Portal del Angel 15*). **Oysho** (*Pelai 46*) has tangas, tops and things to lounge in. Other chains with branches all over town are **Mango**, which is a cut above Zara, and **System Action**.

Window shopping can be mouthwatering

Food

The best and freshest is in the markets. (*For other specialities see pp170–71.*)

Jewellery

Freya

Tiny shop in Gràcia bursting with colourful jewellery cheap enough to treat yourself.
Verdi 17.

Hipòtesi

Stylish quality pieces from local designers and frequent exhibitions of foreign talent in this attractive shop, with manageable prices.
Rambla Catalunya 105.

Leather

Leather is still a good deal. Discount clothes shops can be found on La Rambla, while Loewe remains exclusive. Shoes and handbags range from the cheap and cheerful to top designs like Muxart. The pedestrian street Portal del Angel and Portaferrisa which it leads into have a high concentration of shoe shops. Sought-after Camper, the shoe makers from Mallorca, have their own outlets but are also found in other shoe shops.

Camper

Original shoe design, chunky, comfortable and very well made.
Valencia 249.

Loewe

Elegant expensive leather from gloves to full-length coats.
Passeig de Gràcia 35.

Muxart

Shoes, boots and bags that are like works of art.
Rambla de Catalunya 47.

Tascón

Good range of the best shoe manufacturers in small, appealing shop.
Passeig de Gràcia 53.

Markets

Weekly, seasonal and annual markets are traditional, selling everything from goat's cheese to antique books (*see pp150–51*).

Souvenirs and miscellaneous

For Barça football shirts, Spanish dolls or magnetic paella dishes, La Rambla is the place. For more alternative gift ideas or mementoes try the following:

La Botiga de la Virreina

Barcelona-inspired classy souvenirs from Gaudí 'pavement tile' soap to Miró mouse mats.
La Rambla 99.

Casa Oliveres

One of the few traditional lace shops remaining.
Dagueria 11.

Cereria Subirá

Candles in all shapes and sizes in this candle shop with a history going back to 1762.
Baixada Llibreteria 7.

Gràfiques El Tinell

In the shadows of the cathedral, an old print shop selling cards, engravings and

ex-libris stickers.
Freneria 1.

MACBA (contemporary art museum) shop
Stylish trinkets and inspiring books.
Plaça dels Angels 1.

La Pedrera shop
Classy souvenirs with a predominantly Gaudí theme.
Provença 261–265.

Sports
Decathlon
Sports equipment at affordable prices including rental of bikes, rollerblades and skis.
Plaça Vila de Madrid 1; also in L'Illa.

Traditional fashion
Shops to visit for their charm:

Alonso
Small *modernista* shop crammed with fans, gloves and shawls.
Santa Anna 27.

La Manual Alpargatera
Traditional rope-soled sandals in wide range of styles and colours made on the spot.
Avinyó 7.

Obach
Classic hat shop from the 1920s, now run by the third generation.
Call 2.

Department stores
El Corte Inglés
Still going strong, Spain's main department store where everything can be found. The supermarket is high quality and well stocked with national and imported goods. The branch in Portal del Angel specialises in sports, books and music.
Plaça Catalunya 14; Av Diagonal 617.

Shopping malls
Ever on the increase, exhausting but air conditioned and practical if you are short of time.

Diagonal Mar
The newest shopping centre, and the nearest to the beach, has the major shops found in town.
Diagonal 3–35.

L'Illa
The most sophisticated of them all, designed by Rafael Moneo.
Diagonal 545–557.

El Triangle
One whole corner of the square was taken over to build this. Worth visiting for FNAC, a multi-level book, music and computer store. Open until 10pm.
Plaça Catalunya.

Passeig de Gràcia and Diagonal are for elegant shopping

Despite increasingly frenzied lifestyles and the growth of the hypermarket culture, Barcelona's fidelity to Mediterranean street life and to good eating is reflected in its wonderful and numerous food markets. Each of the city's neighbourhoods has its own municipal indoor food market, and *cuina de mercat* – cuisine using fresh seasonal produce from the market – is a genre of its own developed into a first-rate culinary art by creative chefs.

The market to end all markets, of course, is the famed Boqueria (also known as Mercat de Sant Josep), the inner sanctum of Barcelona's food universe, where the top chefs buy their produce early in the morning. Soaring 19th-century iron architecture provides a cathedral-like setting for this cornucopia of colour and bustle, a feast of sounds and sights and smells.

Several neighbourhood markets are worth a visit, and morning is the best time. The renovated Mercat de Santa Catalina in the Old Town has re-opened as a 'designer market' and should not be missed. By contrast, the Mercat de la Llibertat in Gràcia is small, squashed, intimate and utterly authentic. The food markets also contain bars and bakeries, cooked food and organic produce, and most are surrounded by street stalls, always good for a browse and a bargain. Sant Antoni (the only market in the Eixample built according to Cerdà's

original plan) vies with the Boqueria and Catalina for the distinction of being the oldest.

Seasonal markets are also an institution, in particular the picturesque Fira de Santa Llúcia, held during the run-up to Christmas in the Plaça de la Catedral where locals flock to buy hand-made crib-figures, Christmas trees and other traditional trappings.

Barcelona also has a number of traditional outdoor markets such as the popular secondhand book fair on Sunday mornings at the Mercat de Sant Antoni, which also offers magazines, video games, pins and related

paraphernalia. Sunday morning is also a must for stamp and coin enthusiasts at the market in the Barri Gòtic's imposing Plaça Reial, while at weekends there is an art fair in the Plaça Sant Josep Oriol.

The wondrous assortment of junk and jumble at Barcelona's well-loved flea market, Els Encants, is another institution, and makes a change from the dizzy heights of leading-edge design. If you are really after bargains, make sure you get there early in the morning (many stalls pack up at lunchtime) and watch out for

pickpockets. On Thursdays the antiques and bric-a-brac people set up shop under white canopies opposite the cathedral. Relatively new is the weekend antiques and bric-a-brac fair on the waterfront, at the bottom of the Rambla. Have a good rummage – or retire to refuel and watch the human comedy at one of the many strategic café terraces.

Opposite and above: Whether you shop at La Boqueria (left) or your local market, the produce is at its freshest and best

Entertainment

If you really do need more than the free entertainment on the streets, the changing spectacle of La Rambla or the musicians playing Bach or Blues around the cathedral in the Gothic quarter, to say nothing of the spontaneous Capoeira sessions down by the seafront, or the Andean music on Plaça Catalunya, then read on. There is plenty on offer, from fringe to mainstream, from guitar festivals to festivals of ancient music.

Festival of the Sea

Check local listings, including the weekly magazine *Guia del Ocio*, the daily press and the official Barcelona city agenda at *www.bcn.es*. The English-language magazine *Metropolitan* is available free in various hotels, bookshops, the Palau de la Virreina, bars and cafés.

Nightlife

Trendy bars go in and out of fashion before you can say Jordi Labanda. The

The many cinemas offer a wide choice of films, some in original language

only solution to getting to the hippest spots is to follow the crowd. Try the up-and-coming areas around Joaquín Costa and Ferlandina, just beyond the MACBA (contemporary art museum); also the Old Town in and around Plaça Reial, Plaça George Orwell and Avinyó (*see also pp76–7*). Some favourites are listed here:

Almirall
Laid-back generation in a *modernista* setting dating from 1860.
Joaquín Costa 33.

Benidorm
As kitsch as the name suggests, but cool.
Joaquín Costa 35.

Café Royale
Sophisticated lounge-bar with good music; relaxing.
Nou de Zurbano 3.

Glaciar
A bustling cathedral of a bar with great atmosphere.
Pl Reial 3.

Live music/dance

There are speciality venues but many places have a fusion of styles – a live concert until 1am then DJ sounds, for example. A jazz club will sometimes play flamenco. Check local listings for programmes. Here are some well-established night spots:

Bikini

Just celebrated its 50th anniversary though now in new venue. Good selection of live music.
Deu i Mata 105.

Cibeles

Traditional dance hall turned trendy.
Córcega 363. Tel: 932 720 910.

Harlem Jazz Club

Nothing pretentious about this intimate jazz club that runs the Festival de Jazz of the Old Town every year.
Comtessa de Sobradiel 8.
Tel: 933 100 755.

Jamboree

Long-established jazz club revived in the 1990s has good contemporary programming.
Plaça Reial 17. Tel: 933 017 564.

London Bar

Jazz, blues, Brazilian, plus cabaret and circus acts in a *modernista* setting.
Nou de la Rambla 34. Tel: 933 185 261.

Luz de Gas

Old music hall. Pretty location for jazz and blues concerts.
Muntaner 246.

La Paloma

If you go nowhere else, be sure to spend an evening in this 'Palace of Dance'.
Tigre 27. Tel: 933 016 897.

Razzmatazz, Sala 1

Almogàvers 122. Tel: 933 208 200.
www.salarazzmatazz.com

Razzmatazz, Sala 2 y 3

Apart from concerts, becomes the Loft Club at 1am at weekends.
Pamplona 88. www.theloftclub.com

Sala Apolo

Nou de la Rambla 113.

Los Tarantos

Flamenco is not indigenous to Catalonia so beware of tourist traps – but Los Tarantos has one of the most authentic flamenco shows. Show begins at 10pm. Book in advance if possible.
Plaça Reial 17. Tel: 933 183 067.

Pubs

Nearly every district has its Irish pub now, but the majority are in the Old Town, as well as some other pubs. Very popular when important football matches are being played. Here are just a few:

The Clansman

This one is Scottish. Check the malts.
Vigatans 13.

Fastnet

A cross between a Barceloneta café overlooking the port and a pub serving English food.
Passeig Joan de Borbó 22.

John Martin
Wide selection of draught Belgian beer.
Ases 16.

P. Flaherty
Brunches and a large screen for
unmissable finals.
Plaça Joaquim Xirau.

The Quiet Man
Live music, Guinness, Irish of course.
Marquès de Barberà 11.

Cinema
Most popular commercial films
are dubbed into Spanish or Catalan,
but there are several cinemas which
specialise in *v.o.* (*versión original*) and
show films in the original language.

A new Filmoteca (film theatre) is due to
open in the Rambla del Raval offering
less commercial films. These cinemas,
listed below, tend to have the most
interesting film selection. Also check the
listings in newspapers or magazines,
where it will identify whether a film is
being shown in its original version. The
CCCB regularly holds film festivals of
documentaries, shorts or independent
productions.

Renoir Floridablanca
*Floridablanca 135. Tel: 902 221 622.
www.entradas.com*

Verdi and **Verdi Park**
Both have good programming and
multi-screens.

Billboards everywhere announce forthcoming events

Verdi: Verdi 32. Tel: 932 387 990.
Verdi Park: Torrijos 49. Tel: 932 387 990.

Yelmo Cineplex Icària
In the Centre de la Vila shopping centre
in Vila Olímpica. 15 screens. Sessions
begin at 11am and at weekends there
are 1am sessions.
Salvador Espriu 61. Tel: 902 220 922.

Theatre
With the resurgence of the Catalan
language, most plays are in Catalan.
Occasionally theatre companies from
other parts of Spain visit. There are
some small English-language theatre
companies who perform on the
alternative circuit. If leading Catalan
company Els Joglars are playing do not
miss them: brilliant, scathing theatre that
can be understood despite the language.
Also worth catching are Els Comediants
(very colourful visual theatre) and the
hilarious Cubana company from Sitges.

Mercat de les Flors
A mixed programme often including
more visual theatre, new techniques,
mime etc, so worth checking out. Often
the venue for foreign companies.
Lleida 59. Tel: 902 101 212.
www.mercatflors.com

Teatre Nacional de Catalunya
Excellent standard of theatre,
monumental venue, mostly Catalan.
Their dance programme is worth
watching out for, in summer months.
Plaça de les Arts 1. Tel: 933 065 700.

Tivoli
Charming old theatre. Often has
flamenco shows, visiting stars and more
accessible productions. Well worth
checking out.
Casp 8. Tel: 934 122 063.

Opera
Gran Teatre del Liceu
Tickets for next season (which begins in
September) go on sale in July, but there
are usually some available throughout
the year, or cancellations on the day of
performance. Purchase through
Servicaixa (*see box on p157*) or
www.liceubarcelona.com, or at the ticket
office located in the theatre. *See also
pp82–3.*
La Rambla 51–59. Tel: 934 859 913.

The Tivoli is one of the city's oldest and prettiest
theatres

Classical music

The concert halls have a busy repertoire complemented by different festivals which often take place in the same venues: Festival de Guitarra, Festival de Jazz, Festival de Música Antiga (ancient music). Concerts are occasionally held in the CCCB (*Montalegre 5*), the Caixa Forum on Montjuïc and also in the churches Santa Maria del Mar, Santa Maria del Pí and Sant Felip Neri, all in the Gothic quarter.

L'Auditori

Sophisticated new concert hall near the National Theatre.
Lepant 150. Tel: 932 479 300.

Palau de la Música Catalana

Worth going whatever the concert for the experience of this wild *modernista* music hall designed by Domènech i Montaner.
Sant Francesc de Paula 2.
Tel: 932 681 000.

Major international films are usually dubbed into Spanish or Catalan (*see p154*)

Ballet and dance

The Liceu opera house has a short ballet season, and some visiting companies perform in other theatres. Modern dance can be seen in the Mercat de les Flors, Teatre Nacional (*see p155*) or at L'Espai (*Travessera de Gràcia 63. Tel: 934 143 133*).

Rock concerts

Barcelona is a favourite stopping place for most European tours, from heavy-metal bands to ageing legends from the 1960s. Mega concerts take place in the Palau Sant Jordi on Montjuïc, or in one of the outdoor stadiums. Tickets available through promoters (check listings), record shops in Tallers (just off La Rambla) and FNAC in El Triangle center in Plaça Catalunya. Book online (depending on the promoter) at *www.bbvaticket.com* or *www.ticktackticket.com*

World music

Increasing number of tours of world music artistes and an annual festival in the Caiza Forum. Favourite venues are La Paloma, Sala Apolo, Bikini, Palau de la Música (*see p153 for addresses*).

Casino

Gran Casino de Barcelona. *Marina 19–21. Tel: 932 257 878.*

Bullfighting

Plaza de Toros Monumental. Not for the faint-hearted, nor the politically correct, and what is more not even true to Catalan culture, but for anyone who wants to investigate this side of Spanish culture the only bullring still open in Barcelona is worth a visit. The Monumental was built early in the 20th century as its decorative, tiled façade suggests. Bullfighting season is from April to October. Out of season it is often used by visiting circuses. *Gran Via 747. Tel: 932 455 802.*

TICKET SALES

Many theatres, cinemas, concert halls and other shows centralise their ticket sales through two main telephone agencies:

Tel-Entrada

Tel: 902 101 212. www.telentrada.com. (Caixa de Catalunya savings bank)

Servicaixa

Tel: 902 332 211 or with credit card in Servicaixa machines found in some branches of La Caixa savings bank.

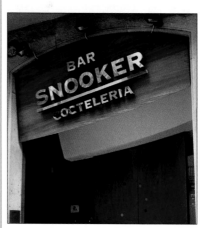

A designer bar complete with snooker table

Children

Travelling with children in Barcelona is relatively easy as Catalans adore them, and small children are still *los reyes de la casa* – in other words the 'kings' or centre of the household. They are welcomed in restaurants, indulged in shops and markets, and often found playing in plazas until late at night, particularly on hot summer evenings or during the different fiestas of Barcelona.

Several companies offer organised bike tours

The free entertainment for kids is boundless. If your visit coincides with one of the many fiestas you have hit the jackpot – huge papier-mâché figures, *gegants*, come out and parade the streets along with mythical beasts and fire-spitting dragons. Processions with

La Rambla street artist

municipal brass bands on horseback, people on stilts and colourful floats tour around the city. Extra fairgrounds mushroom all over the place.

Even without fiestas children love all the spectacles on La Rambla – magicians, statues, clowns, puppets. Activities are often organised for them in the Rambla del Raval, the Plaça de la Catedral or public parks. Check the *infantil* section in local listings for any special events.

The beaches Barceloneta and Nova Icària have climbing frames like spiders' webs and behind Platja Nova Mar Bella is a *half*, as they call it here, for skateboarders and roller bladers. Windsurfboards can be rented on the beach.

The best park for children is the Ciutadella (*see pp102–7*), with a duck pond, rowing boats, a small games park for the tiny, spontaneous drumming sessions at weekends, and of course the zoo – always a hit. Nearby in Passeig de Picasso 40 you can rent a family bike made for four, or individual ones. The Collserola woods (*see pp122–3*) are great for rambles and picnics.

Aquàrium
Situated on Port Vell, in the Maremagnum complex, this huge aquarium delights kids, especially the sharks. There are also specimens from cold and tropical river waters, penguins, piranhas and alligators. The aquarium has more than 50 interactive items.
Tel: 932 217 474.
www.aquariumbcn.com.
Open: daily 9am–9pm.

Cable car
A great trip for everyone, though adults usually get more anxious than kids. Unimaginable peace as you glide over the harbour to the Torre Sant Sebastià, which now has a swish restaurant at a great height. Be sure to choose a clear day for the spectacular views.
Torre de Jaume I, Moll de Barcelona.

The zoo in the Ciutadella is always a success with kids

Family concerts
The Caixa Forum, L'Auditori and El Liceu opera house all have excellent music programmes for children on Saturday and Sunday mornings. See local listings. The CCCB, Fundació Joan Miró and Teatre Poliorama also have cultural programmes tailored for children at weekends.

Golondrinas
These charming wooden pleasure boats originated in the 1888 Exposition and are still going strong. Take a quick trip to the sea wall and back, glimpsing the luxury cruise ships and the giant container vessels in the industrial port. More fun than the newer catamaran which goes out to sea and to the Olympic Port.
Moll de Drassanes, near Columbus monument. Tel: 934 423 106.

Science museum (Cosmo Caixa)
Wonderful, entertaining museum for all the family, now reopened after extensive building work, converting it into one of the best of its kind in Europe. Special section for 3–6-year-olds. *See p135.*

Zoo de Barcelona
Get there early to see the dolphin show (twice a day). Plenty of wildlife to see, horses to ride on and a large adventure playground.
Parc de la Ciutadella.
Tel: 932 256 780. www.zoobarcelona.com.
Open: daily 10am–7.30pm. Closes earlier in winter according to daylight.

Sport and Leisure

Not surprisingly, another area where the Olympic Games made its mark in the lives of Barcelonans was in sport. A dramatic increase in the number and standard of facilities has opened up a range of possibilities to a wider audience.

Not surprisingly, watersports are popular

Football is a consuming passion for most of the population, male and female. Otherwise, Catalans are not traditionally committed to practising sports, though they love to get out at weekends: skiing in winter, spending time on the beach and in the mountains in summer. Walking is an old tradition that forms part of the Catalan spirit: the *Centre Excursionista de Catalunya* in the Gothic quarter dates back to 1876, and it is common today to see groups of young people going off with backpacks on an excursion.

Organised sports have not been a priority – but now that seems to be changing as Catalans, along with the rest of Europe, seek a healthier lifestyle. The new passion is cycling, which is practised enthusiastically both in and out of the city. Specific cross-country cycling routes have been drawn up all over Catalonia.

Bowling
Pedralbes Bowling
All-American bowling alley in a modern part of town. Good for a rainy day.

A cool spot on a hot summer's day

Avinguda Doctor Marañón 11. Tel: 933
330 352. Open: daily 10am–2am.

Cycling
Filicletos
Child bikes, adult bikes, tandems, family
bikes, child seats, all for rental.
Passeig de Picasso 40. Tel: 933 197 811.

Un Cotxe Menys ('one less car')
Good-quality bikes for rent, and
organised tours.
Esparteria 3. Tel: 932 682 105.

Mike's Bike Tours
Good tours on sturdy American bikes.
Plaça George Orwell. Tel: 933 013 612.

Bicycle rental is also available in various
places and at weekends on Montjuïc as
part of the M Card (*see p93*).

Golf
Golf courses are spreading fast across
Catalonia. Within comparatively easy
reach of Barcelona are the following
two courses:

Sightseeing by bicycle

El Prat
A premier course near the airport. Clubs can be hired.
El Prat de Llobregat. Tel: 933 790 278.

Club de Golf de Sant Cugat
Pleasant spot just behind Barcelona, only five minutes' walk from the FGC station (20 minutes from Plaça Catalunya).
Sant Cugat del Vallès. Tel: 936 743 908.

Horse riding
Hipica Sant Cugat
Just outside Sant Cugat. Courses for beginners or day treks in the Collserola hills. Call in advance.
Finca la Palleria, Av Corts Catalanes, Sant Cugat. Tel: 936 748 385. Bus: A4 from FGC station.

Ice skating
Skating Pista de Gel
Large rink fairly central in Eixample.

Roger de Flor 168. Tel: 932 452 800.
www.skatingbcn.com

Swimming
Piscinas Bernat Picornell
Treat yourself to a swim in an Olympic pool. During Grec Summer festival they hold a swim + film season at night.
Av de l'Estadi 30–49. Tel: 934 234 041.
www.picornell.com

Banys Sant Sebastià
Huge indoor and attractive outdoor pools right on the beach. One of Barceloneta's first swimming pools totally rebuilt in the 1990s.
Plaça del Mar 1. Tel: 932 210 506.

Tennis
Centre Municipal Tennis Vall d'Hebron
The Vall d'Hebron, in the foothills of the Collserola range but easy to reach, was another important Olympic centre in 1992. Twenty-four courts

Petanca is one of the oldest, most entertaining spectator sports...

available to the public, but cannot be reserved.
Passeig Vall d'Hebron 178–196.
Tel: 934 276 500. www.fctennis.org.
Metro: line 3 Montbau.

Water sports
Centre Municipal de Vela
Sailing courses for children and adults. Rental of dinghies and windsurfers. Yacht charters for one day or longer.
Port Olímpic. Tel: 932 257 940.

Spectator sports
American football
Barcelona's local team, the Barcelona Dragons, has a great following. Games are played in the Olympic stadium in Montjuïc.

Basketball
Second only to Barça the famed football team, Barça the basketball team are very popular, especially since winning the European Cup in 2003. Part of Fútbol Club Barcelona, they play in the Palau Blaugrana.
Aristides Maillol 12–18. Tel: 934 963 600.
www.fcbarcelona.com

Football
If you get a chance to see a match in Camp Nou, take it (*see pp132–3*). Difficult to get tickets for a match with arch rivals Real Madrid, but lesser matches should be possible.
Aristides Maillol 12–18. Tel: 934 963 600.
www.fcbarcelona.com

Motor sports
Major racing car and motorbike events take place in the Circuit Catalunya in Montmeló, near Granollers.
Tel: 935 719 700. www.circuitcat.com

Petanca
Generally known as *boules* in other parts of Europe, this is the game played by old men in berets. Watching these characters and their technique is a peaceful way to spend an evening. Catch them in most public parks, or along Passeig Lluis Companys, near Arc de Triomf.

Tennis
The Reial Club de Tenis is an exclusive club where the annual Conde de Godó tournament is played.
Bosch i Gimpera 5. Tel: 932 037 852.

...and one of the newest, American football

Food and Drink

With a staggering 3,000 restaurants as well as innumerable bars and cafés which almost without exception serve something to eat, Barcelona offers wonderful food in surroundings for all seasons: convivial old taverns, sunny terraces, museum courtyards, the seafront and even the tip of the pier.

Trendy or traditional, the choice is infinite

A great many of the most emblematic restaurants are clustered in the Gothic Quarter and the Raval, with Barceloneta and the Olympic Port being a must for seafood and the sheer pleasure of eating outdoors, with a soothing view over the Port Vell to Montjuïc or out to sea. Many seafood restaurants offer a selection of tapas called *pica-pica* including crispy-fried vegetable titbits, sardines and croquettes to be dipped into piquant Romesco sauce.

Gràcia, too, is full of eating places, many of them very inexpensive as they are more off the beaten tourist track. While there are restaurants from other regions of Spain such as Galicia and the Basque country, the best bet is to go for Catalan–Mediterranean cuisine, or *cuina de mercat* or *cocina de mercado* (*see pp150–51*), which uses whatever is in season at the local market. Increasingly cosmopolitan, alongside more traditional French and Italian establishments, Barcelona has a growing number of restaurants from across the world, including Greek, Lebanese, Mexican, Thai, Chinese, Japanese and Brazilian. The choice for vegetarians is constantly

improving too. Catalonia also has its own version of fast food in the form of the *entrepà* or *bocata* (sandwich), a long fresh crusty loaf stuffed with ham, omelette, salad, tuna etc. This is the fare offered by local chains such as Pans & Company.

Mealtimes

Lunch, the main meal of the day, is served at the earliest from about 1.30pm, with peak time from 2 till 4pm. Most restaurants in all price ranges offer a surprisingly economical *menú del dia* or set lunch, with even the most basic (just over €6) offering a choice of starter, main course of meat or fish, and dessert plus drink.

For *berenar* or *merienda*, an afternoon snack taken at around 4 or 5pm, try a *granja* (milk bar) or one of the famous *pastisseries* (pastry shops). The *forn* (bakery) is also an institution. More and more of these places have reinvented themselves as stylish little cafeterias, and they are delightful for breakfast, elevenses and afternoon snacks, or for scrumptious pastries and sandwiches to take away to see you through to a late dinner from 9pm. Restaurants usually do not offer set menus for dinner, so be prepared to pay more – or 'do tapas' (*see pp172–3*). It is advisable to book in advance at some of the more upmarket restaurants, particularly for Fridays and weekends.

Wine
The Catalan wine industry is one of the most important in Spain, with a number of official DO regions (*Denominación de Origen*, the Spanish equivalent of the *Appellation Contrôlée*) such as Alella, known for its white wines, Penedès, the home of *cava*, and Priorat. Eating in Barcelona is a good opportunity to try out lesser known wines from the *carta de vins* (wine list).

WHERE TO EAT
The following constitute only a very small selection of eating places worth trying in this food-loving city. The focus is on Catalan and Mediterranean cuisine and seafood. The star ratings are guidelines and refer to an average à la carte meal per person. The set lunch (including drink of wine, beer, water or soft drink) offered by most restaurants is usually much cheaper.

★   Less than €25
★★   €26–50
★★★   € over 50

Catalan
7 Portes ★
Founded in 1836, a true classic. One of the best places for rice dishes. Booking essential.
Pg Isabel II 14 (Barceloneta).
Tel: 933 193 033.

Agut ★★
Dating from the 1920s, this place is typical Barcelona. For a really hearty meal and Catalan 'gastronomic monuments' such as cod with grilled peppers and garlic sauce.
Gignàs 16 (Barri Gòtic).
Tel: 933 151 709.

Can Culleretes ★
Founded in 1785, full of character, plastered with old photos of famous visitors. Long menu of robust traditional dishes (wild boar, goose and so on), as well as a lighter seafood menu. Very inexpensive set lunches on weekdays, very popular, very crowded.
Quintana 5 (Barri Gòtic).
Tel: 933 173 022.

El Glop ★
Informal, homely, slightly rustic air. Booking recommended.
Sant Lluis 24 (Gràcia). Tel: 932 137 058.

A typical dish, prawns with salad

El Pa i Trago ★★
Typical Catalan fare in convivial
atmosphere: red-and-white checked
tablecloths, farm-implement décor
and convivial atmosphere.
Parlament 41 (Sant Antoni).
Tel: 934 411 320.

Via Veneto ★★★
Catalan cuisine with fresh market
produce. One of Barcelona's premier
restaurants.
Booking recommended.
Ganduxer 10 (Les Corts).
Tel: 932 007 244.

Creative
Appetitus ★
Original dishes at reasonable prices.
Very pleasant.
Paris 162 (Eixample). Tel: 934 194 933.

Iposa ★
Brilliant for really tight budgets.
Wide range of interesting dishes with

The Mediterranean terrace café is a wonderful
invention in a medieval square...

international inspiration, including
vegetarian. Tables by the gardens
behind the Boqueria market.
Floristes de la Rambla 14 (Raval).
Tel: 933 186 086.

Jaume de Provença ★★★
Creative chef Jaume Barguès enjoys well-
earned prestige for his original variations
on traditional Catalan cuisine with the
finest quality ingredients. Gourmet
menu offered. Booking essential.
Provença 88 (Eixample).
Tel: 934 300 029.

Semproniana ★★
A whimsical break from style and design,
with its non-matching furniture and
ceramic plates, spectacular old chandeliers
and other flea-market finds. Inventive and
delicious food at reasonable prices. The
star of the dessert menu is the pure
chocolate Delirium Tremens.
Rosselló 148 (Eixample).
Tel: 934 531 820.

Seafood
Botafumeiro ★★★
An institution and the very peak of
sophistication for Galician cuisine. Huge
variety of the choicest, freshest seafood,
rice and noodle dishes and sumptuous
bar. Classy and worth every euro.
Gran de Gràcia 81 (Gràcia).
Tel: 932 184 230/932 179 642.

Can Costa ★★
Genuine fish and seafood cuisine,
excellent paella and squid. Sunny terrace
with sparkling view over the Port Vell.
Pg Joan de Borbó 70 (Barceloneta).
Tel: 932 215 903.

...or on the waterfront

La Oca Mar ★★
Located right at the tip of the breakwater, this ship-shaped restaurant has all-round views of the Med. Excellent seafood and *cuina de mercat*. *Nova Mar Bella, Espigó Bac de Roda (Poblenou/Seafront). Tel: 932 250 100.*

Suquet de l'Almirall ★★★
One of the most interesting seafood restaurants, blending tradition and innovation. Perfectly prepared paella, or try a selection of mini portions of the chef's suggestions. One of the best wine cellars in town. Booking recommended.
Passeig Joan de Borbó 65 (Barceloneta). Tel: 932 216 233.

Xiringuito Escribà ★★
Looks right out over the beach, with sunny terrace. Delicious fish dishes, and one of the city's best dessert selections from the famed Escribà *patissier* family.
Av Ronda Litoral 42 (Beach). Tel: 932 210 729.

Mediterranean
Nao Colon ★★
Near the waterfront, delicious Mediterranean cuisine with Italian, French, Catalan and North African influences. Music at night.
Av Marquès de l'Argentera 19 (El Born). Tel: 932 687 633.

La Provenza ★
Much celebrated for imaginative Mediterranean cuisine with lots of fresh vegetables, fish and wonderful sorbets. Booking recommended.
Provença 242 (Eixample). Tel: 933 232 367.

The Plaça Sant Josep Oriol is a favourite for coffee or an evening drink

Tragaluz ★★

Savour the freshest of Mediterranean ingredients combined in amazingly inventive ways. The place is bathed in light from the glass roof (this is what the name means). Designed by Olympic whizzo Mariscal. Booking essential.
Ptge de la Concepció 5 (Eixample).
Tel: 934 870 621.

Cuina de mercat
Bilbao ★★

Authentic Mediterranean diet and atmosphere. Well-loved local favourite serving whatever is in season, fresh and simply cooked in traditional style. Home-made desserts and very good wine list.
Perill 33 (Gràcia). Tel: 934 589 624.

Can Jaume ★

A century-old tavern cheerfully offering cheap traditional fare in an otherwise terribly upmarket street.
Pau Casals 10 (Sarrià–Sant Gervasi).
Tel: 932 007 512.

Special settings
Flash Flash ★

Unique 1960s-looking place specialising in *tortillas* (omelettes) with every conceivable filling. Never closes.
La Granada del Penedès 25 (Gràcia).
Tel: 932 370 990.

Fundació Miró ★

Eat international while enjoying panoramic views of the city and contemporary sculpture in the adjoining garden.
Fundació Joan Miró (Montjuïc).
Tel: 933 290 768.

L'Hivernacle ★

The romantic 19th-century iron and glass tropical plant house is a truly delightful place for a drink, snack or meal.
Passeig de Picasso (Parc de la Ciutadella).
Tel: 932 954 017.

La Llotja de les Drassanes ★★

Eat well in this superb 13th-century building, in an ambience of art and classical music.
Museu Marítim, Av de les Drassanes
(Raval). Tel: 933 026 402.

La Venta ★★

For a breath of mountain air, lovely terrace and imaginative Catalan-French cuisine.
Plaça Dr Andreu 1 (Tibidabo).
Tel: 932 126 455.

Vegetarian
Comme-Bio ★

The vegetarian's paradise. With ecological wines.

*Gran Via de les Corts Catalanes 603
(Eixample). Tel: 933 010 376.*

Juicy Jones ★
Very full set menu. Excellent vegan food
with fresh market produce, worldwide
influences.
*Cardenal Casañas 7 (Barri Gòtic).
Tel: 933 024 330.*

Tapas
De Tapa Madre ★
The highest quality ingredients make
this one of the city's most popular tapas
bars. Also Castilian 'market' cuisine.
Fresh juices for breakfast, sunny
pavement tables.
*Mallorca 301 (Eixample).
Tel: 934 593 134.*

La Gran Bodega ★
For an authentic tapas experience
untouched by trendiness. Thousands
of tapas and authentic décor.
*València 193 (Eixample).
Tel: 934 531 053.*

Pastisseries
Escribà ★
Barcelona's monumental *modernista*
pastry shop and café. Gorge on the locally
renowned patissier family's sandwiches
and canapés, cakes and chocolates amidst
mosaics and floral décor.
La Rambla 83 (Liceu). Tel: 933 016 027.

Mauri ★
An all-time favourite for afternoon tea:
staggering array of canapés, dainty
sandwiches.
*Rambla Catalunya 102 (Eixample).
Tel: 932 151 020.*

Drinks
Boadas ★
Barcelona's oldest cocktail bar, founded
in 1933 by the father of the present
owner who brought his cocktail-mixing
skills from Cuba. Unique atmosphere
for a pre- or post-dinner drink. Try the
mojito, Hemingway's favourite.
Tallers 1 (Rambla). Tel: 933 188 826.

La Vinya del Señor ★
One of the few places where you can try
different wines by the glass, along with
tiny snacks like olives and slivers of the
finest Iberian ham.
*Plaça Santa Maria 5 (Barri Gòtic).
Tel: 933 103 379.*

Pause for a snack in the middle of the harbour
in the Maremagnum complex

GOOD THINGS TO BUY

For picnicking, what more could you want than a Mediterranean ploughman's lunch: fresh bread, a selection of olives and cheese, washed down with red wine? There's fresh fruit on sale everywhere all year round, too. Or gorge on real ice cream from a branch of Dino's (see below): they sell scores of flavours and will pack your selection into a takeaway isothermic container.

For taking home, possibly the first things that spring to mind are virgin olive oil, wine, cava, moscatel and conyac – look out for Pedrera-chimney-shaped bottles at classy grocers. But if your luggage space is limited there are many other excellent vacuum-packed foods which take up minimal room – serrano ham, sausages (chorizo, llonganissa), Mallorcan sobrasada and even salt cod. Nuts, herbs and handmade chocolates are also good buys. Look out for hexagonal chocolate Gaudí tiles.

Around Christmas time, a delicious easy-to-pack gift is the festive sweet turrón. Go for the real artisanal stuff at a reputable pastry shop. Or how about the 'signature' aceites aromáticos (aromatic oil) by chef Ferran Adrià (see pp38–9) and the Borges company, for sprinkling on food or creating tangy new sauces?

If you can carry heavy parcels home, treat yourself to an earthenware cooking pot or a cast-iron plantxa so you can reproduce some of the healthiest food in the world. Fascinating but fragile are glass cruets with the vinegar container, sometimes shaped like a bunch of grapes, inside the oil container. While design supremos like Vinçon sell stylish utensils, the old shops in Gràcia like Soriano's (see below) can turn up some gems.

Where to shop for food

Casa del Bacalao
The 'house of cod' sells salted and dried cod with no additives. This is the place to buy the raw material to take home: they will vacuum-pack it for you.
Comtal 8 (Barri Gòtic).

Casa Gispert
Wonderland of nuts, dried fruit and coffee.
Sombrerers 23 (Barri Gòtic).

Colmado Quílez
Wonderful grocery store, a monument in itself: walls lined from floor to ceiling with cans and bottles from the five continents, hams, cheeses, alcohol and cava. Mouthwatering.
Rambla de Catalunya 63 (Eixample).

Dino
Traditionally made ice cream in myriad flavours.
Pg Gràcia 33, Pg Gràcia 4, Rambla 54, Pg Juan de Borbón 23.

Ferreteria Soriano
Wonderful old-fashioned store selling traditional utensils like earthenware dishes, special plates for turning Spanish omelettes, drinking flasks, wineskins, asparagus baskets, paella pans and cruet sets.
Gran de Gràcia 53 (Gràcia).